INSTANT POT DUO EVO PLUS COOKBOOK

EASY & DELICIOUS INSTANT POT DUO EVO PLUS RECIPES FOR FAST AND HEALTHY MEALS

(BEGINNERS FRIENDLY)

ELIZABETH GREEN

ISBN: 978-1-950284-93-1

DISCLAIMER

Please note, the information contained in this book, are for educational purposes only. Every attempt has been made to provide accurate, up to date and reliable complete information. By reading this document, the reader agrees that under no circumstances are we responsible for any losses, direct or indirect, which are incurred as a result of the use of the information contained in this document, including but not limited to errors, omissions or inaccuracies.

Table of Contents

Table of Contents...3

INTRODUCTION 7

CHAPTER 1: ABOUT THE INSTANT POT DUO EVO PLUS 9

What is the Instant Pot Duo Evo Plus? 9

Benefits of the Instant Pot Duo Evo Plus 9

Instant Pot Duo Evo Plus Pressure Cooking Tips 10

Instant Pot Duo Evo Plus Commonly Used Function Keys 11

Safety Pressure Cooking Tips 12

CHAPTER 2: INSTANT POT DUO EVO PLUS BREAKFAST RECIPES 17

Chia Berry Crepes 17

Lentils and Poached Eggs 18

Avocado Toasts With Egg 19

Streusel Coffee Cake 20

Mini - Blueberry-Almond French Toast Casserole 21

Chocolate Cinnamon Roll Fat Bombs 21

Bulgar Pilaf 22

Pressure Cooker Carnitas 23

Instant Pot Cajun Shrimp Boil...23

Molten Chocolate Balsamic Cake with Gelato 24

CHAPTER 3: INSTANT POT DUO EVO PLUS STOCKS & BROTH RECIPES 26

Instant Pot Chicken Broth 26

Instant Pot Pork and Chicken Bone Broth 27

Instant Pot Low Carb Beef Bone Broth 28

Homemade Pressure Cooker Turkey Stock 29

Leftover Turkey Bone Broth 30

Instant Pot Chicken Stock...30

Vegetable Broth...31

Shrimp Stock Recipe 32

Easy Fish Broth Recipe 32

Seafood Prawn Stock 33

CHAPTER 4: INSTANT POT DUO EVO PLUS SOUPS, STEWS & SAUCES RECIPES...................................34

Green Chicken Chili...34

New England Clam Chowder...35

Carrot Apple Soup..36

Cream of Jalapeño Soup..36

Creamy Carrot Soup With Warm Spices..37

Beer Cheese Soup..38

Baked Potato Soup...39

Chicken Noodle Soup..40

Tuscan Bean and Sausage Soup...40

Creamy Instant Pot Chipotle Shrimp Soup...41

CHAPTER 5: INSTANT POT DUO EVO PLUS BEANS & GRAIN...43

Quick Soak Dry Beans...43

Homemade Chili With Dried Beans..43

Red Beans and Rice..44

Sausage and White Bean–Stuffed Portobellos.......................................46

Three-Bean Vegetarian Chili..46

Wheat Berry, Black Bean, and Avocado Salad..47

Saucy Pinto Beans...48

White Beans With Smoked Sausage..49

Green Beans With Mushrooms and Bacon..50

Sweet Potato & Black Bean Tacos..50

CHAPTER 6: INSTANT POT DUO EVO PLUS BEEF, PORK & LAMB...52

Easy Beef Stroganoff..52

Ground Beef and Noodle Goulash...53

All-American Pot Roast..53

Lazy Lasagna..54

Beefy Potato Au Gratin...55

Texas Beef Brisket...56

Lamb Korma..57

Simple Tasty Pulled Pork...58

Root Beer Pulled Pork...58

Chipotle-Pork Tacos 59

CHAPTER 7: INSTANT POT DUO EVO PLUS FISH/SEAFOOD RECIPES 60

Steamed Fish with Greens and Miso Butter 60

Fish Taco Bowls 61

Cod Chowder 61

Salmon and Vegetables With Lemon-Butter Sauce 62

Salmon With Red Potatoes and Spinach 63

Halibut With Pineapple Avocado Salsa 64

Tilapia With Pineapple Salsa 65

Simple Steamed Salmon Filets 65

Southwestern Shrimp Soup 66

Sweet and Sour Shrimp 67

CHAPTER 8: INSTANT POT DUO EVO PLUS CHICKEN/POULTRY RECIPES 68

Fall Off the Bone Chicken 68

Chicken Shawarma 69

Southern BBQ Chicken 70

Greens Lemon-Herb Chicken 70

Thanksgiving-Inspired Pulled Turkey 71

Turkey Taco Lettuce Boats 72

Chipotle Turkey and Sweet Potato Chili 72

Buffalo Style Turkey Meatballs 73

Turkey and Stuffing 74

Ma Shu Turkey 75

CHAPTER 9: INSTANT POT DUO EVO PLUS GLUTEN-FREE, VEGETARIAN & KETO DIETS 76

Black-Eyed Peas Summer Salad 76

Chi-Town Italian Beef and Peppers 77

Porcupine Meatballs in Tomato Sauce 78

Vegetarian Chili 78

Lemon Ginger Broccoli and Carrots 79

Coconut Curry Lentil Chickpea Bowls With Kale 80

Buffalo Cauliflower Bites 81

Mac and Cheese 81

Creme Brulee 82

Crab Bisque 82

CHAPTER 10: INSTANT POT DUO EVO PLUS SLOW COOKER RECIPES **84**

Slow-Cooked Whiskey-Molasses Shredded Beef 84

Slow Cooker Giant Chocolate Chip Cookie 85

Slow Cooker German Pancake 86

Slow Cooker Chicken Fajita 87

Slow Cooker Peanut Butter Fudge 87

Kale Slow Cook Spinach and Goat Cheese Lasagna 88

Slow Cook Maple French Toast Casserole 89

Slow Cook Steel-Cut Oatmeal With Apples 89

Chipotle Braised Short Ribs 90

Slow Cook Marinated Flank Steak with Cranberry-Raspberry Salsa 91

CHAPTER 11: INSTANT POT DUO EVO PLUS DESSERTS & CAKES **92**

Maple Bread Pudding 92

Vanilla-Scented Rice Pudding 93

Brandy-Soaked Cheater Cherry Pie 93

Family Size Buttermilk Pancake 94

Pumpkin Pie Custard 95

Raspberry Steel Cut Baked Oatmeal Bars 95

Blueberry Almond Mason Jar Cakes 96

Nutty Brownie Cake 97

Oreo Cheesecake 97

Fudgy Chocolate Cake 98

MEASUREMENT CONVERSIONS & ABBREVIATIONS **100**

When Living on High Altitude 102

ABBREVIATIONS AND ERROR CODES 103

Error Codes and Meaning 104

CONCLUSION **106**

INTRODUCTION

There is always a "but" and "what ifs" in everything we lay our hands on because our wants are simply insatiable. No sooner than we get used to the Instant Pot than we started seeing rooms for improvements. I'm sure you can relate with this point if you've read enough reviews about the Instant Pot series.

Users have whined about lids, leakage, burnt, and all sorts of inadequacies even though they enjoyed using it. Despite having a lot of things to complain about, you still have to give it to the Instant Pot; pressure cooking has been taken to an unprecedentedly high level. Even then, as users' experience has shown, there are still genuine concerns and there are areas that need to be improved upon.

Every new model of the Instant Pot comes with, at least, a special feature that serves as an enhancement to the ones before it. The Instant Pot Brand makers certainly have their ears on the ground and remarkably responsive. They evidently have an active interest in all reviews from real users. They treat these the same way they will customer feedbacks.

That is why they try to factor in the complaints and demands of the users in the new models. So if you're amazed and impressed by the functionality of your Instant Pot and have believed that you've got a perfect cooking companion, more surprises await you. What again?

It's the **Instant Pot Duo Evo Plus**. This is more than just another model of the Instant Pot. It is a new evolution and a complete revolution of pressure cooking. As you will see, it has taken care of all concerns and complaints about the Instant Pot. It has improved upon the convenience, safety, and every other aspects and pro of the pressure cooking.

This is worth devoting a book to. I dare say here that the Instant Pot Duo Evo plus is the combination of all peculiar advantages of the Instant Pot ever produced. Any further enhancement to this product in the future will come from outside this world. You've probably heard about the Instant Pot smart WI-FI, the Instant Pot Ultra, and the Instant Pot Lux. What about the Viva, Max, Duo, and Duo Nova?

The Instant Pot Duo Evo Plus is different from all of these in its features and functions. That is what you'll be reading about in this book.

In the opening section, you will read the description of the Instant Pot Duo Evo plus. You will also come across the benefits of this brand and those of the Instant Pot in general. Safe usage tips of the pot will also be a focus of the chapter. What about overfilling the Instant Pot? The chapter brings that to the fore.

The challenges encountered when the pressure cooker is overfilled when cooking foamy food are addressed also in the chapter. You will also learn about how to cook liquids to appropriate thickness. The chapter elaborates on what to do to avoid minor injuries that usually result from opening the lid.

The next 10 chapters are devoted to the consideration of the various recipes that can be cooked in the Instant Pot Duo Evo plus. About 100 of such recipes are given for readers' tasty delights. And the eBook concludes with how to handle abbreviations conversions.

This book will improve your appreciation for the use of Instant Pot Duo Evo plus as you compare it will other pressure cookers you've ever used or seen.

CHAPTER 1: ABOUT THE INSTANT POT DUO EVO PLUS

What is the Instant Pot Duo Evo Plus?

To be sure, the Instant Pot Duo Evo Plus is a member of the Instant Pot family of pressure cookers. However, being the latest, it has incorporated everything you could ever love about other pressure cookers. It can be referred to as the greatest of them all thanks to some design improvements that it has incorporated and the several new features of it that you'll love.

This latest model of electric pressure cooker by Instant Pot is available in sizes of 6-quart and 8-quart with 9 smart programs that consist of Pressure Cook, Rice/Grain, Steam, Sauté, Slow Cook, Sous Vide, Yogurt, and Bake. Its preset buttons are 8 on the sides. It also has a dial that you can use to customize your cooking to as much as 48 programs.

It's currently the most powerful Instant Pot yet to be designed; far ahead of Instant Pot Max in terms of wattage. Thus, it's going to heat more quickly do the sautéing better. It will also reach pressure more quickly due to its quicker pressurizing.

Benefits of the Instant Pot Duo Evo Plus

The Instant Pot brands didn't just wake up one day and decided to produce yet another brand. The Duo Evo Plus is vastly different from other Instant Pot in the following areas:

1. *Preset buttons:* While many previous models of the Instant Pot have their different button locations and additional presets to the lid with operations of the machines strikingly similar, the new Instant Pot Evo Plus has introduced a lot of major changes to actual parts.
2. *Digital displays:* Another new thing is the display which shows the progress of the cooking and the exact point you are in the pressure. The progress bar will show and will let you determine how much longer the process will take. You don't have to bend over to catch the display light as it is angled for ease of readability.
3. *Redesigned cooking lid:* The lid of the Instant Pot Duo Evo Plus automatically seals when in place. Once you put the lid on, you will hear the jingle and know that it's time to relax. A pressure release switch has also been added which makes it possible for you to release the pressure while you keep your hand at a safe distance and avoid steam injury.
4. *Updated lid fins:* There are little lid holders sitting in the housing. They have been redesigned to be angled in the new model. The holders have also been moved from the sides to be closer to the back. So when stirring the pot, the lid is now out of the way. That's a big difference.
5. *Faster and cuter pressure release:* Thanks to the QuickCool™ technology and the QuickCool™ Tray, the natural pressure release is 50% faster. Your heating can start faster than usual. Apart from this, Duo Evo Plus comes with a steam release cover. This prevents liquid from spitting during quick pressure releases as it usually happens with the previous Instant Pot when cooking high starch foods. Thus, there

is a reduced need for intermittent pressure releases. The sound is also dampened during a quick release.

6. *Inner pot redesigned:* The Instant Pot Duo Evo Plus comes with a new flat-bottom inner pot that is stovetop-friendly. It's great for sautéing. It also has two easy-grip handles which ensure that you can safely move it from one appliance to another. It is Tri-Ply stainless steel that is transferrable to electric stovetop, ceramic, gas, or induction cook-tops.

7. *Bake setting expanded:* This new model has made an enhancement to the bake setting. With its new proofing setting, you have a cheesecake setting and a cake setting. All these are in addition to an entirely new dry baking option. That means you can bake your cake without having water in the bottom of the pot. You just have to select the temperature. It works just like your oven.

8. *Sous vide:* It adds sous vide which is a great enhancement to your cooking. Your guests will be impressed as they taste one of the trends in cooking.

9. *Changing Time and Lever Without Restarting:* If you have to change the cook time and pressure level in the Instant Pot Duo Evo, you don't need to cancel the process and restart. You only need to hold the center dial and wait until it beeps. Then spin it to change the cook time. If it is an adjustment to pressure level, press the center once and make the adjustment.

Instant Pot Duo Evo Plus Pressure Cooking Tips

Understanding a few basic tips about pressure cooking with the Instant Pot Duo Evo Plus will tremendously help you to enjoy cooking with your pot.

Assembling:

1. Position the inner pot in the base unit of the Instant Pot Duo Evo Plus while you have the handles rest in the handle notches.
2. Set up the condensation collector with its edges aligning with the notches that are on the back of the Pot's base unit.
3. Gently slide in the condensation collector until it is completely pushed in. (The condensation collector traps any moisture building up on the rim.)

Opening and Closing the Lid

To close the lid:

1. First position the lid on top of the Instant Pot Duo Evo Plus base unit while the arrow mark pointing to the lid lined up with the small bar above the control panel right corner. You should hear a chime if the volume is turned on.
2. Then turn the lid clockwise; you will hear another chime showing that the lid is closed.

To open the lid:

1. Turn the lid counterclockwise; you hear a chime as you do so.
2. The arrow on it should be aligned with the bar on the base unit.
3. Try to remove the lid by lifting it; it should come up easily
4. If the lid doesn't come up freely, wiggle it back and forth till the suction releases.

Pressure Release

These are basic pressure release methods for the Instant Pot Duo Evo Plus:

1. *Natural Pressure Release/Natural Release:* This is used for foods that take longer to cook. Even after the pressure cooking is complete, the built-up pressure continues to cook the food. Also referred to as NPR or NR, it is the process of allowing the pressure to release on its own. That means you decide to wait until the float valve comes down on its own. You may have to wait for anything between 10 to 45 minutes, depending on the food you're cooking, the quantity, and the length of pressure cooking time. After the lid float has dropped, turn the lid counterclockwise to open. You will hear a chime.

2. *Quick Release:* This stops the cooking process immediately by letting out the pressure that has been cooking the food. You do this at the end of the pressure cooking time. Also called QR, you do it by moving the steam release switch from the "Seal" position to the "Vent" position. Steam will spew out from the steam release vent. The float valve will drop once all the steam has been released. It's time to turn the lid counterclockwise to open. Once you hear a chime, lift the lid to open.

3. *10-minute or 15-minute Natural Pressure Release:* This is what you use on occasions your recipe directs a natural pressure release but you are pressed for the time. You can also use it when you believe that allowing a full natural release would overcook your food. You do this by allowing just 10 or 15 minutes of natural pressure release and then do a quick release of the remaining pressure.

4. *Quick Release in Short Bursts:* Foods than can be frothy and messy, such as soups, pasta, and oatmeal can be taken through this release method even though the recipes state that it should be quick release. You do this by moving the steam release switch to the "Vent" position for just a second and then return it to the "Seal" position. This process will be repeated until the steam spewing out becomes less forceful. At this point, you can do a normal quick release for the remaining steam to come out.

5. *Faster Natural Pressure Release With QuickCool:* This method adopts the use of ice to lower the pressure. It speeds up natural pressure release by about 50 percent. It's used for tender-crisp vegetables and delicate fish and the likes. In principle, you add the ice tray to the metal part of the lid and the float valve will drop. It works pretty like the traditional way of pouring cold water on the lid of the stovetop pressure cooker so that you will be able to more easily reduce the pressure.

Instant Pot Duo Evo Plus Commonly Used Function Keys

Apart from the 8 function buttons assigned to the 8 or 9 smart cook programs (each with an assigned button), there are other function keys that are commonly used on the Instant Pot Duo Evo Plus. They are Pressure Cook | Custom option, Sauté, Keep Warm, Start, and Cancel.

Below are their functions:

1. *Pressure Cook | Custom option*

- It's assumed that the display will be on "Off", so press the knob once to turn it on.
- Once it's on, press the "Pressure Cook" button.
- Adjust the knob until "Custom" starts blinking.
- Once "Custom" is blinking on the display, press the knob to confirm the setting.
- Then the time, such as 00:10 for example, will be blinking.
- Turn the knob clockwise (to 00:15 for example) or anticlockwise (to 00:05 for example) to reach your desired pressure cooking time.
- Press Start.

2. *Sauté*

- Once you press "Sauté", the sauté time will start blinking on the display (showing for instance 00:30 which indicates 30 minutes)
- Turn the knob clockwise (to 00:45 for example) or anticlockwise (to 00:20 for example) to reach your desired sauté time.
- Once the desired time is reached, press the knob to confirm your selection.
- The temperature level will start blinking on the display starting from LE 1 to LE 6 as the custom temperature level. Turn the knob to the desired temperature level.
- Then press the "Start" button to activate the sauté function.

3. *Keep Warm*

The "Keep Warm" button is what you will press to activate and deactivate the Keep Warm function. When you want your food to keep warm after it's been pressure cooked, turn the "Keep Warm" function on. The icon of a steaming pot will be displayed at the top.

4. *Start*

You press the "Start" button to activate the selected function or preset. (For example, you can select "Sauté". But to activate it you have to press "Start." The message "On" will appear on the display.

5. *Cancel*

You press "Cancel" when you want to end the selected function. And the message "Off" will appear on the Instant Pot Duo Evo Plus display panel.

Safety Pressure Cooking Tips

For you to cook safely with the Instant Pot Duo Evo Plus, a lot of safety considerations have been included in its design to eliminate many common errors causing injuries to users and damages to foods. Consider the following 10 proven safety mechanisms together built in the pot.

1. *Steam Release:* This releases excess pressure by allowing the steam to spew out through the steam release valve or handle.

2. *Anti-Block Shield:* This is a stainless steel cover that prevents food particles from gaining access to the steam release pipe and causing blockages.

3. *Safety Lid Lock:* Lid of the Instant Pot Duo Evo Plus is designed to automatically lock when the cooker is pressurized. This prevents the cooker from opening when the pressure is built. Users shouldn't try to force the lid of a pressurized cooker open while pressure is still high.

4. *Lid Position Detection:* This cooker will not initiate any cooking program if the lid is not yet in a safe position for pressure cooking.

5. *Automatic Temperature Control:* This feature regulates heating so that the inner pot is kept within a safe temperature range as set for the cooking program.

6. *Overheat (Burn) Protection:* The cooker will detect overheating and prevent burn by automatically lowering the heat output. A burn may result when:

   - The inner pot is not deglazed after sautéing and the food particles remain stuck to the bottom;
   - The volume of the liquid in the pressure cooker is not sufficient for the cooking;
   - There is partial contact between the inner pot and the heating element; and
   - There is a heat distribution issue that affects the inner pot, such as an accumulation of starch on the bottom of the inner pot.

7. *Automatic Pressure Control:* This is what helps to maintain working pressure levels. Once the pressure *exceeds* pressure level limits, it suspends heating.

8. *Electrical Fuse:* This cuts power off whenever the electrical current exceeds safety voltage limits.

9. *Thermal Fuse:* This too cuts power off whenever the internal temperature is higher than safety limits.

10. *Leaky Lid Detection:* If for any reason (such as when sealing ring is improperly installed or steam release handle is left in "Venting" instead not "Sealing" position), steam is leaking from the lid, the cooker will not pressurize; loss of steam may cause food to burn. Also, this pressure cooker monitors the pre-heating time. It will lower the heat output if it doesn't reach working pressure within 40 minutes.

Dos and Don'ts

Although there are a lot of built-in safety features in the pressure cooker, it behooves on the user to abide by some common-sense precautions when cooking, such as:

Dos
   ✓ Check and see that the anti-block shield, steam release pipe, and float valve are all clean and not clogged.

✓ Ensure that your hands and face are away from the steam release mechanism during the pressure release.
✓ Be extra careful when doing a quick-release of frothy foods such as oatmeal, pasta, and soups among others. Pressure release in short burst is the best for these kinds of foods.
✓ Open the lid only when you're sure that the float valve has dropped.

Don'ts

❖ Don't touch any hot surface, mainly all the stainless steel parts. Rather use the handles to move the pressure cooker and/or the inner pot.
❖ Don't place the Instant Pot on or in close proximity to an electric or gas burner.
❖ Don't move an Instant Pot that is under pressure.
❖ Don't fill an Instant Pot beyond 2/3 full.
❖ Don't fill it beyond ½ full when cooking foods that expand such as beans, rice, and pasta.
❖ Don't open the lid until the Instant Pot is depressurized (you know this when the float valve is down).
❖ Don't use the lid of another model of Instant Pot on the Duo Evo Plus.

Safest Way to Open the Lid

Don't try to open the lid when the float valve is still up.
Don't try to open the lid if it's locked and can't be easily opened.
Don't ever force the lid open.

If the inner pot adheres to the lid when opening the lid, there is a vacuum due to cooling. The vacuum can be released by moving the quick release switch to the "Vent" position.

Overfilling the Instant Pot Instant Pot Duo Evo Plus

Avoid overfilling the Instant Pot Duo Evo Plus as it will affect the pressure build-up inside it. You might eventually have a mushy meal or a meal that doesn't cook properly. To help you avoid this is the line on the inner pot that indicates the maximum level of the food to be cooked in it at once.
If your food exceeds the maximum line, your pressure release knob can be clogged since the food and liquid from an overly-full Instant Pot will get sucked up inside.
As a general rule, you should not fill your Instant Pot beyond the two-thirds line on the inner cooking pot. If you're dealing with foods such as beans and lentils that expand while cooking, stay below half full.
In case you accidentally overfill your Instant Pot, don't panic. If it ever comes to pressure, the best way to safely open it and stay clean is to use natural pressure release.

Using Quick Release for Foamy Food or When Cooker is Overfilled

Many new users make the mistake of using quick pressure release when they're a pressure cooking foamy foods, such as applesauce, beans, or grains. This can result in the splattering of food through the Venting Knob all over the Instant Pot. The same thing will happen if the pot is overfilled.

The solution is to use a natural pressure release. However, as mentioned earlier, if the recipe calls for quick pressure release as many usually do, use the quick release in short burst and gradually. Then later do a quick release of the remaining pressure. You can be sure the pot won't retain the pressure that will likely overcook your meal.

Cooking Liquid: Avoiding Too Thick Food or Cooking Without Enough Liquid

As you have seen, there is a minimum liquid requirement for any food you want to cook. So follow the recipe to avoid too thick food. If it's too thick, your pot will not have enough steam to generate pressure.

As a general rule, you can start with at least 1 cup when cooking. Don't add thickeners such as arrowroot, cornstarch, flour, potato starch when pressure cooking. Add any of these only after the pressure cooking cycle.

On the other hand, there's a limit to the quantity of liquid that can be used if you don't want to end up with too watery messy food. Too much liquid in the Instant Pot will overcook your food as it will increase the time it takes to come to pressure and to release pressure. It will also affect the taste as it will dilute the seasoning.

It will also help to stick with the recommended amount of liquid for pressure cooking if your recipe does not specify otherwise. Generally,

A 3-Quart Instant Pot pressure cooker requires 1 cup (8 oz) of liquid

A 6-Quart Instant Pot pressure cooker requires 1 ½ cups (12 oz) of liquid

An 8-Quart Instant Pot pressure cooker requires 2 cups (16 oz) of liquid

When referring to liquids, if not specified, the recipes usually refer to water-based liquids such as broth, cooking sauces, juice, stock, as well as beer and wine. Oils and oil-based sauces generally don't contain enough water to make up for the liquid volume requirement. If you're using condensed cream-based soups or thick sauces, add suitable liquid to thin them.

Grain-to-Water Ratios

While pressure cooking grains in the Instant Pot Duo Evo Plus, the following is the recommended water ratio:

Grain/Rice   **Water Ratio**

White or Brown Rice	1:1 cup
Quinoa	1:¾ cups
Oatmeal	1:3 cups
Risotto	1:2 cups plus additional wine to taste
Porridge	1:10 cups

CHAPTER 2: INSTANT POT DUO EVO PLUS BREAKFAST RECIPES

There is no gainsaying the fact that breakfast tastes better when taken through the Instant Pot, especially if it's Duo Evo Plus. Any recipe prepared in such a pot will be a great one to break your overnight fast as you have every ingredient and nutrient retained and compacted in your moderately cooked meal.

It can be anything from crepes from berries, to eggs, avocado, coffee and any favorite that you feel good starting your day with.

Take note, though, some of the recipes here are by no means restricted to breakfast alone; they are all-time meals. Most of them are actually good for the diabetic. So there are no reasons for anyone to worry about anything along that line. And the recipes are mostly American.

Chia Berry Crepes

Loaded with fiber are those teeny chia seeds. They become gelatinous when mixed with liquids. Thus, sauces and dressings have got a nice thickener. This is an important factor to have in your mind while incorporating more fiber into your meal to change its texture.

Total cook time: 30 minutes.

Ingredients
- 1 cup frozen blueberries
- 1 cup frozen raspberries
- ½ cup water plus 1 tbsp. water (to be divided)
- 2 tsp. chia seeds
- 2 tsp. cornstarch
- 3 tbsp. powdered sugar (to be divided)
- 1/8 tsp. almond extract
- 4 premade crepes (such as Melissa's)
- 1 cup plain Greek yogurt (2%, such as Fage)

Instructions
1. Mix a half cup of water with the berries and the chia seeds in the Instant Pot Duo Evo Plus. Have the lid tightly sealed and the valve closed. Select "Pressure Cook" and turn the knob to set the cook time to 1 minute. Then use a quick pressure release. After the pressure is all gone and the pin has dropped, carefully remove the lid.
2. Mix the cornstarch with the remaining 1 water in a small bowl and stir very well until the cornstarch is dissolved.
3. Press the "Cancel" button and then the "Sauté" button. Adjust it to the custom temperature. Then stir in the cornstarch mixture to the berries. Sauté and bring to a boil for 1 minute, or until slightly thickened. Turn off the heat.
4. Stir in 2 tablespoons of the sugar and almond extract. Pour the berry mixture into a medium bowl and wait for about 15 minutes for it to slightly cool.

5. Equally spoon the berry mixture down each crepe center. Fold all ends over to overlap slightly. Then spoon the remaining 1 tablespoon of sugar into a fine-mesh sieve. Allow it sprinkle evenly over each crepe. Add the yogurt as a topping on each crepe in an equal amount while serving warm or chilled.

Yield: 4 servings.
Nutritional content per serving: Total fat: 3.5g, Carbs: 28g, Fiber: 4 g, Protein: 8 g, Cholesterol 10 mg, Calories: 170.

Lentils and Poached Eggs

It needs to be stated here that lentils and poached eggs are also a meal for any time and not just breakfast. However, thanks to the Duo Evo, your eggs can be poached to be enjoyed with lentils as you will see in this diabetic another recipe.

Total cook time: 32 minutes.

Ingredients
- ¾ cup dried brown (or green) lentils (to be rinsed and drained)
- 2 dried bay leaves
- 3 cups water (to be divided)
- 3 tbsp. extra-virgin olive oil
- 1 tbsp. fresh parsley (finely chopped)
- 1 lemon grated zest and juice
- ½ tsp. salt (to be divided)
- Nonstick cooking spray
- 4 eggs
- 4 cups baby spinach
- ¼ tsp. black pepper

Instructions
1. Combine the lentils and bay leaves with 2 cups of water in your Instant Pot Duo Eva Plus. Have the lid tightly sealed and the valve closed. Set the IP on "Pressure Cook" for 7 minutes.
2. Meanwhile, whisk together the oil, parsley, lemon zest plus juice, and ¼ teaspoon of salt in a small bowl and set aside. Also, coat 4 (6 oz. size) ramekins with cooking spray. Then crack 1 egg into each ramekin and set aside.
3. After 7 minutes of pressure cooking, quick-release the pressure and wait for the pin to drop. Then carefully remove the lid and discard the lentil water and bay leaves. Once drained, return the lentils to the Instant Pot with the spinach. Add ¼ teaspoon of salt and toss until the spinach is just wilted. Then, divide the mixture between 4 soup bowls and cover to keep warm.
4. Pour the remaining 1 cup of water into the pot and place the 4 ramekins on a trivet inside the pot. Tightly seal the lid and have the valve closed. Press the "Cancel" button to reset the "Pressure Cook" to 1 minute. Once it beeps, use a natural pressure release for 1 minute and then do a quick pressure release of the remaining pressure. Once the pin drops, gently remove the lid and then transfer the ramekins into a tray and drain off any excess water that may have

accumulated. Run a knife carefully around the outer edges of each egg so that they can be easily released from the ramekins.

5. Top each serving of the lentils with the eggs and spoon equal amount of the oil mixture on each serving. Then sprinkle with black pepper.

Yield: 4 servings.

Nutritional content per serving: Total fat: 15g, Total Carbs: 22g, Fiber: 9 g, Protein: 16 g, Cholesterol 185 mg, Calories: 140.

Avocado Toasts With Egg

This is a great time-saving recipe as most of its cooking is done while the eggs are cooking and cooling. It'll definitely cut down on the total time while presenting a great meal.

Total cook time: 32 minutes.

Ingredients
- 3 cups water (to be divided)
- 4 large eggs
- 2 cups ice cubes
- 2 avocados (to be peeled and roughly mashed)
- 1 jalapeno (to be seeded, if desired, and minced)
- 3 tbsp. light mayonnaise
- 3 tbsp. lemon juice
- 1 tsp. Dijon mustard
- ¼ tsp. salt
- 4 oz. multigrain Italian loaf bread (to be cut diagonally into 12 thin slices, then lightly toasted)
- ½ cup diced tomato
- ¼ cup chopped fresh cilantro
- 2 tbsp. minced red onion
- 1 lemon (to be cut into 4 wedges)

Instructions
1. Pour 1 cup of water into the Instant Pot and add a steamer basket with the eggs arranged. Tightly seal the lid have the valve closed. Set the "Pressure Cook" button to 7 minutes.
2. Meanwhile, add the remaining 2 cups of water and the ice cubes in a medium bowl. Also combine the avocado, jalapeño, lemon juice, mayonnaise, mustard, and salt in a small bowl and stir together
3. When the pot beeps, use a quick pressure release. Once the valve drops, remove the lid carefully and immediately place the eggs in the ice water leave for 3 minutes. Then peel the eggs and cut in half. Remove 4 of the egg yolk halves and add the remaining to the avocado mixture. Mash until all yolks have blended well with the mixture, appearing slightly lumpy. Finely chop the egg whites and set aside.

4. Spread the avocado mixture on the slices of bread by dividing it evenly between the slices. Top with the egg whites, cilantro, onion, and tomato and serve immediately with the lemon wedges squeezed over all.

Yield: 4 servings.

Nutritional content per serving: Total fat: 17.0g, Total Carbs: 24g, Fiber: 8 g, Protein: 11 g, Cholesterol 95 mg, Calories: 280.

Streusel Coffee Cake

This is a great deal! Pressure-cooking your coffee cake is quite easy and quick. But you don't have to go through the stress of heating your oven, especially on a hot summer day.

Total cook time: 60 minutes.

Ingredients
- 2 1/3 cups baking mix (all-purpose, to be divided)
- ½ cup brown sugar (packed, to be divided)
- ½ tsp. ground cinnamon
- 4 tbsp. cold butter (to be divided)
- 1 large egg
- 2/3 cup water

Instructions
1. Grease a nonstick fluted tube pan (preferably 7-inch). Then, add 1/3 cup baking mix and 1/3 cup brown sugar and combine with cinnamon in a small bowl. Cut in 2 tablespoons of butter, using a pastry blender or two knives, until crumbly. Add half of the streusel mixture to the bottom of the prepared pan. Meanwhile, add together the remaining baking mix and sugar in a medium bowl. Cut in the remaining butter until crumbly.
2. Thoroughly whisk egg and water in a measuring cup or bowl and the dry ingredients mixture. Stir until just combined. Then, pour half of the batter over streusel mixture in a pan and sprinkle with the remaining dry streusel. Also, top with the remaining batter.
3. Pour 1 cup of hot water to the inner pot, place the steam rack in the pot and then the pan on the rack. Tightly close lid in place and have the steam release handle turned to "Sealing." Set the Instant Pot to "Pressure Cook", temperature to LE 6 and time to 25 minutes.
4. Once the pot beeps signaling that the cooking is done, press "Cancel" and wait for 10 minutes of natural pressure release. Then turn the steam release handle to "Venting" for the quick release of the remaining pressure. Once the float valve drops, carefully remove the lid. After checking the tester inserted in the center and it's discovered that more cooking time is needed, repeat the process for 3 minutes then do a quick release of the pressure.

Yield: 6 servings.

Nutritional content per serving: Total fat: 18.g, Total Carbs: 15g, Fiber: 9 g, Protein: 14 g, Cholesterol 105 mg, Calories: 200.

Mini - Blueberry-Almond French Toast Casserole

The introduction of tangy blueberries and crunchy almonds has taken the French toast to another dimension. Nevertheless, it remains simple enough to be considered an everyday favorite, breakfast for that matter.

Total cook time: 30 minutes.

Ingredients
- 1 cup whole milk
- 2 eggs
- ¼ cup brown sugar
- ½ tsp. almond extract
- ½ tsp. cinnamon
- 1 cup fresh blueberries (or ½ cup frozen to be thawed)
- 4 thick slices French bread (to be cut into 2-inch pieces)
- Cooking spray
- Powdered sugar (for serving)
- Slivered almonds (for serving)
- Additional blueberries (for serving)
- Maple syrup for (serving, optional)

Instructions
1. Whisk together the eggs, milk, almond extract, brown sugar, and cinnamon in a large bowl until well blended. Then, fold in the blueberries and slices of bread until well coated.
2. Spray a baking dish with cooking spray, and then transfer the bread mixture into the dish. Position the steam rack in the Instant Pot inner pot, add ¾ cup of water and carefully lower the baking dish down to the steam rack. Secure the lid and have the valve turned to the "Sealing" position. Press the "Pressure Cook" button and adjust turn the knob to set the time to 25 minutes.
3. When the pot beeps, do a quick release of pressure and serve immediately or wait to cool a bit.

Yield: 4 servings.

Nutritional content per serving: Total fat: 17g, Total Carbs: 19g, Fiber: 8 g, Protein: 16 g, Cholesterol 100 mg, Calories: 140.

Chocolate Cinnamon Roll Fat Bombs

The ketoers will leap for joy with the mere mention of fat bombs. But wait a minute if you are one! You have a lot to be happy about in a chapter ahead. The fat bombs we have here have no sugar but have chocolate and coconut butter that boosts metabolism.

Total cook time: 10 minutes.

Ingredients
- 2 tbsp. coconut oil
- 2 cups raw coconut butter
- 1 cup sugar-free chocolate chips

- 1 cup heavy whipping cream
- ½ cup Swerve confectioners (or to taste)
- ½ tsp. cinnamon ground (or to taste)
- ½ tsp. vanilla extract

Instructions

1. Start the Instant Pot on the Sauté mode and when hot add the oil to melt. Add butter to the heated oil. When hot, add chocolate chips, cream, Swerve, cinnamon, and vanilla and continue sautéing in the pot. Stir once a while until the mixture reaches the desired smooth consistency.
2. Pour the mixture into 5 silicone mini-muffin molds and freeze. When it has firmed up, serve and enjoy!

Yield: 5 servings.

Nutritional content per serving: Total fat: 32 g, Total Carbs: 15.1 g, Dietary Fiber: 6.8 g, Protein: 4.2 g, Calories: 372.

Bulgar Pilaf

Also called cracked wheat, the Bulgur wheat is a nice alternative to rice that is tasty and high in soluble fiber. The recipe has a flavor that is reminiscent of the Thanksgiving cornbread dressing.

Total cook time: 18 minutes.

Ingredients

- 1 tbsp. olive oil
- 1 tbsp. butter
- 3 tbsp. onion (to be finely chopped)
- 2 tbsp. celery (to be finely chopped)
- 1 cup medium bulgur wheat (uncooked)
- 2 cups chicken broth
- ½ tsp. Italian seasoning
- ½ tsp. table salt
- Lime wedges (for garnishing, optional)
- Chopped cashews (for garnishing, optional)
- Fresh chives (for garnishing, optional)

Instructions

1. Combine olive oil and butter in an Instant Pot and select the "Sauté" function. When the butter melts, add onion and celery and continue cooking. Stir constantly for two minutes and then add bulgur and continue stirring until it's coated with oil. Stir in the broth, Italian seasoning, and salt.
2. Press "Cancel" to turn the cooker off. Cover the Instant Pot with the lid and lock it in place with the steam release handle turned to the "Sealing" position. Select the "Rice/Grain" function and cook at low pressure for 12 minutes. When the pot beeps, use the Quick Pressure Release to remove the lid. Fluff the pilaf with a fork.
3. Serve with any of the garnishes (if desired).

Yield: 5 servings.

Nutritional content per serving: Total fat: 12g, Total Carbs: 10 g, Fiber: 18 g, Protein: 10 g, Cholesterol 80 mg, Calories: 90.

Pressure Cooker Carnitas

These strips of braised pork can also serve a sumptuous breakfast if cooked in the Instant Pot Duo Evo Plus. With the help of orange juice, it makes a very great tasty meal.

Total cook time: 55 minutes.

Ingredients
- ¼ cup Fiesta pork rub
- 1 cup white onion (to be chopped)
- ½ cup cilantro (to be chopped)
- 16 oz. Green chile tomatillo salsa (Specialty Series)
- ½ cup orange juice (freshly squeezed)
- 1 tbsp. oil (to taste)
- Taco mini corn tortillas (to be warmed)
- 12 oz. mango pico de gallo

Instructions
1. In the Instant Pot, add seasoning to the pork and stir to coat. Then select the "Sauté" function to brown. Add the next four ingredients (from onion to orange juice) to the Pot.

2. Select the "Pressure Cook" setting and turn the knob to set the timer for 50 minutes. Close the lid and place and ensure that the valve is turned to "Sealing". Then, press "Start." When the countdown reaches zero and the pot beeps, use the quick release of the pressure method. Carefully open the lid when all the pressure is gone. Use two forks to shred carnitas and fry with oil in a non-stick skillet until crispy.

3. Serve with tortillas and mango pico de gallo.

Yield: 6 servings.
Nutritional content per serving: Total fat: 23g, Total Carbs: 39 g, Fiber: 9 g, Protein: 29 g, Cholesterol 95 mg, Calories: 90.

Instant Pot Cajun Shrimp Boil

Sausages are easy and take less time to cook and are smart to eat. Thus, on a busy morning, it can readily serve as your breakfast if shrimp is called to the party as you can see in this recipe.

Total cook time: 30 minutes.

Ingredients
- 6 tbsp. butter
- 1 tbsp. Creole seasoning
- 1 ½ cups red chopped onion (about half a large red onion)
- 12 oz. Texas heritage sausage (to be sliced into 1-inch thick pieces)
- 2 lb. baby red potatoes
- 4 ears fresh sweet corn (husks and silks to be removed and to be sliced in quarters)
- 1 ½ lb Texas fresh farm-raised shrimp (to be peeled, deveined)

Instructions

1. Start the Instant Pot on the "Sauté" function. Combine half of butter, half of seasoning, and the entire onion in the inner pot. Sauté until the butter is melt and onions caramelized, usually about 2 minutes. Add the sausage, potatoes, and corn. Close the lid in place with the valve turned to the "Sealing" position pot and set on "Pressure Cook" with the time set for 4 minutes.
2. When the pot beeps at the completion of the cooking time, do a quick release of pressure by manually turning the venting valve, using a wooden spoon to avoid burns from the steam.
3. Meanwhile, add the remaining butter with seasoning in a large skillet. Toss in the shrimp and set the pot to "Sauté" for 3 to 5 minutes, depending on the size of the shrimp, to cook through.
4. Coat the potato mixture in shrimp and juices, stir well and serve immediately.

Yield: 6 servings.
Nutritional content per serving: Total fat: 23g, Total Carbs: 38 g, Fiber: 6 g, Protein: 29 g, Cholesterol 225 mg, Calories: 230.

Molten Chocolate Balsamic Cake with Gelato

Chocolate cake too can be a very mealy recipe on a breakfast considering the contribution from Gelato. It's fast and crisp. So if you love cakes for your breakfast, I invite you to read with a special interest a chapter ahead.

Total cook time: 35 minutes.

Ingredients
- ½ cup salted butter (to be melted)
- 4 large eggs
- 1 ½ cups coconut sugar
- 1 tbsp. vanilla extract
- 1 tbsp. aged balsamic vinegar (nice quality only)
- 1 cup flour
- ½ cup baking cocoa
- 2 cups water

Instructions

1. Lightly butter a round baking dish or spray and set aside. Combine butter, eggs, sugar, vanilla, and vinegar in a large bowl. Beat together, using an electric mixer or whisk, until smooth. Also, sift flour and cocoa and add to the egg mixture. Beat briefly to smooth.

2. Pour water into the inner pan of the Instant Pot and place the trivet in the bottom. Then pour batter into prepared pan and cover with foil. Firmly close the lid and have the vent valve turned to the "Sealing" position. Set the pot to "Pressure Cook" and adjust the time to 25 minutes with the temperature on high setting. Press "Start." When the cook time has elapsed, allow 15 minutes of natural pressure release and manually release the remaining pressure.

3. Serve warm with gelato and fresh berries. Drizzle with balsamic vinegar if desired.

Yield: 6 servings.
Nutritional content per serving: Total fat: 20g, Total Carbs: 55 g, Fiber: 33 g, Protein: 8 g, Cholesterol 165 mg, Calories: 170.

CHAPTER 3: INSTANT POT DUO EVO PLUS STOCKS & BROTH RECIPES

We are used to cooking with store-bought stocks and broth and are fine with them. Granted, it takes a lot of time to prepare these cooking liquids that will be suitable for our food. Nevertheless, the Instant Pot Duo Evo Plus has come to the rescue making it easier for us to do this.

The broth is the cooking liquid flavored with the like of fish, meat, and vegetables. It is generally clearer and not simmered for such a long time as stock. Stock, on the other hand, is a cooking liquid that has been simmered for a long time with bones and is usually richer in color.

You can also hear about bone broth which is made with roasted bones and simmered for a long time for products like gelatin and trace minerals to be released. And the bones will crumble or be broken easily. Of course, there is vegetable broth. Check all that out in this chapter.

Instant Pot Chicken Broth

Let's start you off with the chicken broth as a perfect easy addition to your recipe or meal prep game. It affords you a function for those considered as kitchen scraps from other recipes. It will add extra flavor and nutrition to your meal.

Total cook time: 1 hour 35 minutes.

Ingredients
- 2 ½ lb. roasted chicken carcass
- 6 medium carrots (to be roughly chopped)
- 6 stalks celery (to be roughly chopped)
- 1 medium yellow onion (to be roughly chopped)
- 4 cloves garlic (to be smashed)
- 6 sprigs rosemary (fresh)
- 6 sprigs thyme (fresh)
- 1 tbsp. whole black peppercorn
- 2 tbsp. apple cider vinegar
- 12 cups cold water

Instructions
1. Add all ingredients, including the chicken bone, in the inner pot of the Instant Pot and stir well to combine. Start the pot on the "Sauté" mode and bring to boil on high temperature. Continue cooking until all impurities foam to the surface. Carefully skim off the foam on top with a large spoon.
2. Cover the lid tightly in place and turn the venting valve to the "Sealing" position. Set the pot to cook on high pressure for 60 minutes. Once it beeps to signal the end of the cooking, do a quick release of pressure by switching the valve to the "Venting" position (watch your hand; it shouldn't be over the switch release.) After the hot steam has all spewed out and all the pressure has been released, carefully remove unlatch the lid.

3. Use a fine-mesh sieve with cheesecloth lining to strain the broth and wait for it to cool completely. Store the broth in an airtight container for up to 6 days in the refrigerator or 30 days in the freezer.

Yield: Yield: 6 cups

Nutritional content per serving: Carbs: 7g, Fiber: 3g, Calories: 32.

Instant Pot Pork and Chicken Bone Broth

Quite popular in North America in recent years, bone broth has been known for its various health benefits, including boosting immune system thereby offering protection against common cold and flu, improving digestion by strengthening the your digestive tract, improving allergies, and supporting hair, joints, skin, and nail growth because of its high collagen contents.

Total cook time: 3 hours.

Ingredients
- 2 ½ - 3 lb. bones (a combination of pork and chicken in ratio 75:25)
- 5 - 6 chicken feet
- 2 onions (with the outer layers, to be roughly diced)
- 2 celery stalks (to be roughly diced)
- 2 carrots (to be roughly diced)
- 2 bay leaves
- 2 garlic cloves (¼ oz., to be crushed)
- 1 tsp. whole peppercorn
- 8 cups cold water
- 2 tbsp. fish sauce (or light soy sauce)
- Fresh or dried herbs (of your choice)
- 1 tbsp. apple cider vinegar
- 1 tbsp. olive oil

Instructions

1. Press the "Sauté" button on your Instant Pot and press the knob to select "Start" after setting the temperature to high. Once it's hot, add 1 tablespoon of olive oil in inner pot and brown each side of the bones for about 4 minutes. This may be done in two batches. Add half cup of cold water to completely deglaze the pot by using a wooden spoon to scrub all flavorful brown bits.
2. Pressure cook the chicken feet and the rest of the ingredients by tightly closing the lid, having the valve turn on the "Sealing" position and pressure cook at a High Pressure for 2 hours. When the countdown reaches zero and the pot beeps, wait for 45 for natural pressure release before carefully opening the lid.
3. Using a colander or mesh strainer, strain the bone broth and discard the solids. Set aside to cool. Then use a fat separator to skim off the fat. Alternatively, you may place the bone broth in the fridge so that the fat will rise to the top and form a layer of gel. You can then skim the fat layer with a spoon which is an indicator of rich gelatin content in the bone broth.

4. Season the broth with salt (optional, to taste) and drink it directly or use it in place of stock. It can be refrigerated for 3 - 5 days. It can be frozen for up to a year for the best quality.

Yield: 12 servings.

Nutritional content per serving: Total fat: 2g, Carbs: 1g, Fiber: 3g, Protein: 0 g, Cholesterol 11 mg, Calories: 54.

Instant Pot Low Carb Beef Bone Broth

The Instant Pot beef bone broth is packed with nutrients that promote health. Typically, making bone broth can take multiple days. However, the Instant Pot has sped up the process such that you can make delicious beef bone broth in only a couple of hours. Beef bone broth is wonderful for cooking or drinking hot all alone.

Total cook time: 3 hours.

Ingredients
- 4 lb. beef soup bones and short ribs (the package should contain some marrow bones)
- 1 shallot cut (to be quartered)
- 1 head garlic (to be cut in half)
- 2 stalks (to be cut in half)
- 1 bunch Italian parsley
- 2 bay leaves
- 1 tbsp. apple cider vinegar
- 1 tsp. black pepper
- 1 twig fresh thyme (1 tsp. dried)
- ½ tsp. coriander seeds
- 12 cups water and more as to start

Instructions
1. Fill your Instant Pot insert with water about ¾ full and start it on the "Sauté" to water to a boil. Add the bones when the water is boiling and boil 20 minutes. With the impurities from the bone now released, drain the liquid and rinse off both the bones and Instant Pot inner pot.
2. Arrange the bone, shallot, and garlic on a sheet pan and roast at 450° F for about 30 minutes each side. Add the roasted bones, garlic, and shallot to the Instant Pot together with any drippings from the pan. Add the rest of the ingredients and 12 cups of water.
3. Close the lid in place and have the pressure valve turned to the Sealing. Press the "Pressure Cook" button and set to cook the broth for 2 hours. After the cooking time, allow an hour of natural pressure release. Then carefully open to strain the broth into a large container. Quicken the cooling time by adding a cup of ice to the broth. Then, pour the cool broth into an airtight container and store in the refrigerator for up to 7 days. You can freeze the remaining broth in portions for up to 6 months using a large ice cube tray.

Yield: 12 servings.

Nutritional content per serving: Total fat: 2g, Carbs: 1g, Fiber: 3g, Protein: 0 g, Cholesterol 11 mg, Calories: 218.

Homemade Pressure Cooker Turkey Stock

While some find it challenging to make stocks at home, this homemade turkey stock recipe gives you a reason to make the effort. Why waste the turkey carcass from your holiday feasts when you can make rich homemade turkey stock from it? It can be a great soup base and add depth of flavors to your dishes.

Total cook time: 2 hours 15 minutes.
Ingredients
- 2 ½ lb. roasted turkey bones
- 3 tbsp. olive oil (to be divided)
- 10 cups cold water
- 2 medium onions (keep the outer layers, to be diced)
- 3 (½ lb.) celery stalks (to be diced)
- 3 (½ lb.) carrots (to be diced)
- 6 (1 oz.) garlic cloves (to be minced)
- 2 bay leaves
- 1 tsp. whole black peppercorn
- A pinch dried rosemary
- A pinch dried sage
- A pinch dried thyme
- 1 tbsp. apple cider vinegar (Optional)

Instructions
1. Toss turkey bones and carcasses with 2 tablespoons of olive oil and roast in a preheated oven at 450°F until browned; for about 40 minutes. Meanwhile, press the "Sauté" on your Instant Pot and use the knob to adjust to the "More". Your pot will indicate when it's hot.
2. Add 1 tablespoon of olive oil to the hot pot and then add diced onion. Sauté for about a minute until softened. Then add minced garlic and continue sautéing for 30 seconds more until fragrant. Add celery and carrot and continue sautéing for about 10 minutes or until the vegetables are slightly browned. After 5 minutes of sautéing, add in black peppercorn, the herbs, and 2 bay leaves.
3. Deglaze by adding a half cup of cold water to the Instant Pot and using a wooden spoon to scrub all the brown flavorful bits off the bottom of the pot.
4. Add the roasted turkey bones and the remaining cold water into the Instant Pot Duo Evo Plus. Now is the time to add apple cider vinegar if you are using it. Tightly close the lid with the valve turned to the "Sealing" position and time set for 60 minutes. Then, cook at High Pressure. When the timer counts down to zero, allow 30 minutes of natural pressure release and quickly release the remaining pressure.
5. Using a fine-mesh strainer, strain the turkey stock through and allow it to cool up to room temperature. After refrigerating overnight, skim the layer of fat off the surface of the stock. You can store it if refrigerated up to seven days and frozen for about 3 months.

Yield: 10 cups.
Nutritional content per serving: Total fat: 4g, Carbs: 6g, Fiber: 2g, Protein: 1 g, Cholesterol 11 mg, Calories: 63.

Leftover Turkey Bone Broth

Still on the turkey. What would you do with your turkey leftovers? Bone broth provides the perfect answer. It's the best way to use up the nutrient-dense and immune-boosting turkey parts.

Total cook time: 2 hours 15 minutes.

Ingredients
- 2 lb. turkey bones
- ½ tsp. sea salt
- 1 tbsp. apple cider vinegar
- 1 celery rib (to be coarsely chopped)
- 1 carrot (to be coarsely chopped)
- ½ onion (to be quartered)
- Scraps from turkey dinner prep (such as carrot peels, celery leaves, etc.)
- Leftover herbs from turkey dinner prep
- 10 cups water (should not be filled beyond 2 inches to the top of the Instant Pot)

Instructions
1. Combine all ingredients in the Instant Pot and select the "Pressure Cook" button (on the Duo Evo Plus). Set to LE 6 and turn the knob to set the timer for 120 minutes. Then press "Start". When the countdown drops to zero, do 60 minutes of natural pressure release until the pin drops down. Alternatively, after about 20 minutes, of natural pressure release, you can carefully do a quick pressure release of the remaining pressure.
2. Pour through a colander to strain while the bone broth is collected in a large bowl or a jar. Toss all solids in the compost and store the pure broth in the refrigerator for up to 7 days or in the freezer for up to 3 months. You can use part of it immediately.

Yield: 8 cups.
Nutritional content per serving: Carbs: 1g, Fiber: 2g, Calories: 53, Calcium: 12mg.

Instant Pot Chicken Stock

Back to the chicken! This time it's the stock. Using the magic of pressure cooking, you can make rich homemade stock with your chicken in no time at all.

Total cook time: 50 minutes.

Ingredients
- 1 chicken carcass (bones from a roasted chicken, alternatively)
- 2-3 cups vegetable scraps (such as carrot peels, celery, garlic, onions, etc.)
- 1 sprig thyme (optional)
- 1 tbsp. kosher salt
- 1 tsp. peppercorns
- 2 bay leaves
- 10 cups cold water

Instructions

1. Set all ingredients in the Instant Pot Evo Duo Plus and lock into place with the vent valve pointing to the "Sealing" position. Press the "Pressure Cook" button and turn to 45 minutes and press "Start" When the countdown drops to zero, allow 30 minutes of natural pressure release. Carefully open the lid when the pin drops.
2. Using a colander or mesh strainer, strain the stock and cool. Use immediately or store for later use.

Yield: 5 cups.

Nutritional content per serving: Total fat: 10g, Carbs: 6g, Fiber: 7 g, Protein: 33 g, Cholesterol 19 mg, Calories: 50.

Vegetable Broth

Even vegetable broth can be easier to make than you imagined. Homemade vegetable broth can be filled with so much healthier flavor than the store-bought since you are in control of the content. The recipe here can be made in an Instant Pot, slow cooker, or regular pot. But let's use the Instant Pot Duo Evo Plus to find a use for the extra vegetable scraps or your frozen vegetables.

Total cook time: 60 minutes.

Ingredients
- 2 (1 lb.) small onions (with the outer layers, roughly chopped)
- 2 (3 oz.) celery stalks (to be roughly diced)
- 2 (7 oz.) carrots (to be roughly diced)
- 2 bay leaves
- 1 (¼ 0z.) dried shiitake mushroom
- 6 (3 oz.) cremini mushrooms (to be roughly sliced)
- 4 (¼ oz.) garlic cloves (to be crushed)
- 1 tsp. whole peppercorn
- 2 tbsp. light soy sauce (not low sodium)
- 8 cups cold water
- Any favorite fresh (or dried) herbs

Instructions
1. Combine all ingredients in the Instant Pot. Close lid in place and have the vent valve turned to the "Sealing" position. Select the "Pressure Cook" button and cook on LE 6 (high pressure) with the time adjusted to 15 minutes. Press start.
2. When the pot beeps to indicate that the pressure cook time is up, wait 15 minutes for natural pressure release and then turn the venting knob to the "Venting" position for the quick release of remaining pressure. Carefully open the lid.
3. Strain vegetable stock, using a fine-mesh strainer and allow it cool to room temperature. Then refrigerate for up to 7 days.

Yield: 10 servings.

Nutritional content per serving: Total fat: 10g, Carbs: 4g, Fiber: 1 g, Protein: 1 g, Cholesterol 19 mg, Calories: 23.

Shrimp Stock Recipe

Many folks are yet to appreciate that seafood broth and stock can also make a remarkable enhancing cooking liquid for soups, stews, or any seafood dishes. Pressure cooking shrimp in the Instant Pot is a great hands-off, very easy way to make any seafood. The resulting stock can be used in the cooking of Cajun and Creole dishes like étouffée.

Total cook time: 50 minutes.

Ingredients
- 4 cups water
- Shells from 2 lb. shrimp
- ½ cup parsley (packed)
- 1 celery stick (to be cut into 1-inch slices)
- 1 onion (to be quartered)
- 2 small bay leaves (or 1 large)

Instructions
1. Add all ingredients in the Instant Pot and stir well to combine. Select the "Pressure Cook" function on the Instant Pot and set to cook on LE 3 (medium pressure) for 30 minutes. Allow natural pressure release until the pin drops.
2. Drain the content of the inner pot by setting a colander in a medium bowl or use a mesh strainer. Then, transfer the broth to a jar and refrigerate for up to 3 days or store for a month in the freezer.

Yield: 4 servings.

Nutritional content per serving: Total fat: 10g, Carbs: 1g, Fiber: 1 g, Protein: 1 g, Calories: 1.

Easy Fish Broth Recipe

The versatility of this recipe is worth a pound. Once done, it can be used as the cooking liquid for many dishes. It will be a source of extra flavors and soup bases. For the sake of health, it can also be taken as a drinking soup.

Total cook time: 55 minutes.

Ingredients
- 1 - 2 fish heads, tails, or collars
- 1 - 2 fish fillets (any white fish is fine)
- 2-3 celery ribs
- ½ onion
- 1-2 carrots
- 1 tsp. thyme
- Salt and pepper (as desired)
- 1 - 2 bay leaves

Instructions
1. Combine all the ingredients in the inner pot of your Instant Pot and add enough water to submerge the ingredients by an inch or two without going over the MAX line. Seal the lid over the pot with the toggle switch turned to the "Sealing" position.

Press the "Pressure Cook" button and set to cook on LE 6. Set the time for 40 minutes and press "Start".

2. At the end of cook time, do a quick release of the pressure carefully and remove the lid. Then, using a large bowl and a colander, strain to sieve off the solid from the liquid and discard the solids. Store the broth in an airtight container in the fridge for 3 days if not using immediately.

Yield: 1 cup.

Nutritional content per serving: Total fat: 2g, Carbs: 1g, Fiber: 1 g, Protein: 17 g, Calories: 94, Cholesterol: 15mg.

Seafood Prawn Stock

Prawn stock that is rich in vegetables contains all essential ingredients. The stock from this can be used as bases for many recipes.

Total cook time: 30 minutes.

Ingredients
- 2 cups prawns
- 1 large carrot
- 1 large onion
- 10 garlic cloves
- 1 stalk celery
- 15 whole peppercorns
- 3-4 liters cold water

Instructions
1. Combine all the ingredients in the Instant Pot and add water up to the 2/3rd mark. Tightly close the lid with the vent valve on the "Sealing" position. Set the pot to "Pressure Cook" mode and to cook on high pressure for 30 minutes. When the cook time is up, do a quick release of the pressure.
2. Strain the using a colander or fine-mesh and remove the prawns and vegetables. Allow it to cool down and store in the fridge until needed.

Nutritional content per serving: Total fat: 0.1g, Carbs: 4.1g, Fiber: 1 g, Protein: 0.6 g, Calories: 20.

CHAPTER 4: INSTANT POT DUO EVO PLUS SOUPS, STEWS & SAUCES RECIPES

Let's now give attention to how soups, stews, and sauces will fare in the Instant Pot Duo Evo Plus. Can pressure cooking them in the pot make a significant difference? It certainly will, even though they've always made nice additions toppings and sides to dishes.

Before the culinary world understands the technology of pressure cooking, it has always been creative with soups. However, the granny's ingenuity can be modernized and enhanced with the current advancement in pressure cooking. She'll proud of you that your Instant Pot Duo Evo Plus has rebranded what she handed down to the coming generation.

Thus, you need to consider what you can do with the examples of recipes you can bring to life in this chapter.

Green Chicken Chili

This chili owes its green color into the combination of poblano and Anaheim peppers. The addition of tomatillos produces a fresh and light-flavored chili. Dressing it up are the crushed corn chips, white cheese such as quesadilla, fresh cilantro, and sour cream.

Total cook time: 45 minutes.

Ingredients
- 2 tbsp. unsalted butter
- 1 medium yellow onion (to be peeled and chopped)
- ½ lb. poblano peppers (to be seeded and roughly chopped)
- ½ lb. Anaheim peppers (to be seeded and roughly chopped)
- ½ lb. tomatillos (to be husked and quartered)
- 2 small jalapeño peppers (to be seeded and roughly chopped)
- 2 garlic cloves (to be peeled and minced)
- 1 tsp. ground cumin
- 6 bone-in, skin-on chicken thighs (2 ½ lbs. in total)
- 2 cups chicken stock
- 2 cups water
- 1/3 cup roughly chopped fresh cilantro
- 3 cans Great Northern beans (to be drained and rinsed, 15 oz. cans)

Instructions
1. Press the "Sauté" button on the Instant Pot and when hot, add butter to melt. Once the butter melts, add onion and cook for about 3 minutes until softened. Add poblano and Anaheim peppers, then tomatillos, and jalapeños. Cook 3 minutes add garlic and cumin. Cook about 30 seconds or until fragrant. Then cancel sautéing.
2. Add the thighs, stock, and water to pot and stir. Tightly close lid and have the steam release set to the "Sealing" position. Select the "Rice/Grain" option and set the timer for 30 minutes. At the end of the cook time, do a quick release of pressure and open lid to stir well. Press the "Cancel" button and transfer the chicken to a cutting board. After carefully removing the skin, shred the meat with two forks.

3. Using an immersion blender, purée the sauce until smooth. Stir in the meat, cilantro, and beans and serve warm.

Yield: Yield: 8 servings.

Nutritional content per serving: Total fat: 10g, Carbs: 19g, Protein: 33 g, Calories: 304.

New England Clam Chowder

Opinions continue to differ about who actually introduced the creamy version of clam chowder to New England. Certain things are sure; it's popular and classic from coast to coast. You can make your chowder meal in an extra special by adding sourdough boule you bought from the bakery, chop off the top of the loaf and hollow out the base. You've made your soup bowl!

Total cook time: 30 minutes.

Ingredients
- 6 tbsp. unsalted butter
- 1 stalk celery (to be chopped)
- 1 medium carrot (to be peeled and chopped)
- 1 medium yellow onion (to be peeled and diced)
- 2 garlic cloves (to be peeled and minced)
- ½ tsp. ground white pepper
- ¼ tsp. dried thyme
- ¼ tsp. dried oregano
- 1/3 cup all-purpose flour
- 4 cups seafood stock
- 1 bay leaf
- 1 lb. russet potatoes (to be peeled and diced)
- 2 cans chopped clams (6 ½ oz. each)
- 2 cups heavy cream
- 1/3 cup chopped fresh chives

Instructions
1. Press the "Sauté" button on the Instant Pot and when hot, add butter to melt. When the butter melts, add celery, carrot, and onion. Stir and cook for about 5 minutes, or until tender. Add the next 4 ingredients and cook for about 30 seconds, or until fragrant. Sprinkle flour overcooking vegetables and stir well. Allow to continue cooking for 1 minute until flour is completely absorbed. Gradually add the stock and whisk constantly until smooth. Next, add bay leaf and potatoes. Stop sautéing by pressing the "Cancel" button.
2. Close lid with the steam release turned to the "Sealing". Then press the "Pressure Cook/Custom" button with the cook time set to 5 minutes. Press "Start."
3. Once the cook time is up, allow 15 minutes of natural pressure release. When pin drops, gently open the lid and stir in clams and cream. While discarding the bay leaf, serve the chowder immediately with chives as a garnish.

Yield: 8 servings.

Nutritional content per serving: Total fat: 39g, Carbs: 19g, Fiber: 1g, Protein: 15g, Cholesterol 11 mg, Calories: 419.

Carrot Apple Soup

Besides all the widely known health benefits of apple, an apple soup is also refreshing. Its perfect taste goes along well the natural sweetness of carrots and cream.

Total cook time: 40 minutes.

Ingredients
- ¼ cup unsalted butter
- 4 medium carrots (to be peeled and finely chopped)
- 2 medium Granny Smith apples (to be cored and chopped)
- 1 garlic clove (to be peeled and minced)
- 1 tsp. grated fresh ginger
- ½ medium sweet onion (to be peeled and finely chopped)
- 1/8 tsp. ground nutmeg
- ½ tsp. dried tarragon
- 3 cup vegetable broth (or chicken stock)
- ¾ cup heavy cream
- ½ tsp. salt
- ½ tsp. ground black pepper
- 3 tbsp. chopped fresh chives

Instructions
1. Press the "Sauté" button on the Instant Pot and when hot, add butter to melt. When the butter melts, add carrots. Stir and cook for about 5 minutes. Add apples, garlic, ginger, onion, nutmeg, and tarragon and cook until fragrant. Stir well and cook for about 2 minutes. Press the "Cancel" button and stop sautéing. Add vegetable broth and stir well.
2. Close lid in place with the steam release valve turned to the "Sealing" position. Press the "Pressure Cook/Custom" button program to cook for 10 minutes. When the timer beeps, allow about 15 minutes of natural pressure release.
3. When the valve drops, carefully open the lid and stir it well. Then, purée the soup until smooth, using an immersion blender. You can alternatively work in batches with a blender. Add cream, salt, and pepper and stir well. Then, sprinkle with chives and serve hot.

Yield: 6 servings.

Nutritional content per serving: Total fat: 19g, Carbs: 13g, Fiber: 2g, Protein: 1 g, Calories: 227.

Cream of Jalapeño Soup

Jalapeño peppers can also be used in an unexpected way. It can make a soup with less spice. All you need is to carefully scrape out the jalapeños ribs before chopping. And for a soup with an additional kick, include some dashes of any favorite hot sauce.

Total cook time: 22 minutes.

Ingredients

- 4 tbsp. unsalted butter

- 8 medium jalapeño peppers (to be seeded and finely chopped)
- 1 medium onion (to be peeled and finely chopped)
- 3 garlic cloves (to be peeled and minced)
- ½ tsp. ground cumin
- ½ tsp. ground coriander
- ½ tsp. salt
- ¼ tsp. ground black pepper
- ¼ tsp. smoked paprika
- ¼ cup all-purpose flour
- 4 cups chicken broth
- ¾ cup heavy whipping cream

Instructions

1. Press the "Sauté" button on the Instant Pot and when hot, add butter to melt. When the butter melts, add jalapeños and onion. Stir and cook for about 6 minutes or until tender. Add the next six ingredients up till and including paprika and stir well. Cook for about 1 minute or until fragrant. Add flour and cook for a minute more, ensuring that all flour is moistened. Stop sautéing by pressing the "Cancel" button. Gradually add broth, stirring and scraping the bottom of the inner pot.
2. Close lid in place with the set steam release valve turned to the "Sealing" position. Press the "Pressure Cook/Custom" button program to cook for 3 minutes. When the timer beeps, allow about 10 minutes of natural pressure release. Then quick-release the remaining pressure.
3. Then, purée the soup, using an immersion blender. You can alternatively work in batches with a blender. Stir in the cream and serve hot.

Yield: 8 servings.

Nutritional content per serving: Total fat: 14g, Carbs: 6g, Fiber: 2g, Protein: 2 g, Cholesterol 11 mg, Calories: 163.

Creamy Carrot Soup With Warm Spices

Carrots and onions together with some spices cooked in the Instant Pot can produce a simple but luxurious aromatic soup. The cleanness and brightness of carrots are usually muted when other vegetables, fruits, or dairy are added. Therefore, plenty of such is not used here. The topping of tart Greek yogurt and pomegranate molasses as a drizzle underscores the natural sweetness of the carrots.

Total cook time: 50 minutes.

Ingredients

- 2 tbsp. extra-virgin olive oil
- 2 onions (to be roughly chopped)
- 1 tsp. table salt
- 1 tsp. ground cinnamon
- 1 tbsp. ground coriander
- 1 tbsp. ground fennel
- 1 tbsp. grated fresh ginger
- 4 cups vegetable (or chicken) broth
- 2 cups water

- 2 lb. carrots (to be peeled and cut into 2-inch pieces)
- ½ tsp. baking soda
- 2 tbsp. pomegranate molasses
- ½ cup plain Greek yogurt
- ½ cup hazelnuts toasted, skinned, chopped
- ½ cup chopped fresh cilantro or mint

Instructions

1. Select the "Sauté" function with the highest heat to heat the oil until shimmering. Add onions to the hot oil and stir. Then, add salt and leave to cook for about 5 minutes for the onion soften. Stir in cinnamon, coriander, ginger, and fennel and cook for about 30 seconds, until fragrant. Stir in broth, carrots, water, and baking soda.
2. Close the lid securely and turn the pressure release valve to the "Sealing" position. Select the "Pressure Cook/Custom" function and cook for 3 minutes. When the timer counts down to zero, quick-release pressure and carefully remove lid when the pin drops.
3. Pureé the soup in blender 1- 2 minutes until smooth; do it in batches. Return pureéd soup to Instant Pot and sauté again on the highest function. Season with pepper and salt to taste.
4. Serve drizzling individual portions with pomegranate molasses while topping with yogurt, hazelnuts, and cilantro.

Yield: 6 servings.

Nutritional content per serving: Total fat: 19g, Carbs: 13g, Fiber: 2g, Protein: 1 g, Cholesterol 11 mg, Calories: 227.

Beer Cheese Soup

Lager or ale beers are arguably the best cheese soups because they don't dwarf the cheese flavor. They rather enhance it with a slightly bitter and nutty sensation. If you garnish the bowls of this soup with crisp bacon or sliced scallions, your palate will be grateful.

Total cook time: 25 minutes.

Ingredients
- 3 tbsp. unsalted butter
- 2 medium carrots (to be peeled and chopped)
- 2 stalks celery (to be chopped)
- 1 medium onion (to be peeled and chopped)
- 1 clove garlic (to be peeled and minced)
- 1 tsp. dried mustard
- ½ tsp. smoked paprika
- ¼ cup all-purpose flour
- 1 bottle lager beer or ale (12 oz.)
- 4 cups chicken broth
- ½ cup heavy cream
- 2 cups shredded sharp cheddar cheese
- 1 cup shredded smoked Gouda cheese

Instructions

1. Select the "Sauté" function on the Instant Pot and when hot, add butter to melt. When the butter melts, add carrots, celery, and onion. Stir and cook for about 5 minutes or until softened. Next, add garlic. Cook for about 30 seconds, or until fragrant. Stir in mustard and paprika. Stir in flour, mix thoroughly to combine, and then cook for 1 minute. Gradually add in beer and deglaze by scraping the bottom of the pot with a wooden spoon. Then, add broth and stir well. Press the "Cancel" button.
2. Close lid in place with the steam release turned to the "Sealing", position. Select, "Pressure Cook/Custom" function and adjust the time to 5 minutes, then press "Start". When the timer counts down to zero, wait for 15 minutes of natural pressure release.
3. Open lid and purée mixture using an immersion blender. Then stir in cream, then the in the cheese and serve.

Yield: 6 servings.

Nutritional content per serving: Total fat: 22g, Carbs: 8g, Fiber: g, Protein: 13 g, Cholesterol 11 mg, Calories: 302.

Baked Potato Soup

This recipe of baked potato-style soup in the Instant Pot transforms common ingredients into the ultimate comfort meal. You'll get all you want in a meal in these loaded baked potatoes in a delicious creamy soup. You're free to customize it with your favorite toppings! Here we entrust it onto the chicken broth to give us the perfect savory soup base! Fast and easy!

Total cook time: 36 minutes.

Ingredients

- 4 slices bacon (to be diced)
- 1 large yellow onion (to be chopped into about 1 cup)
- 2 cloves garlic (to be minced)
- 2 lb. russet potatoes (to be peeled and cut into ½-inch pieces, about 6 cups)
- 4 cups chicken broth
- ¼ cup sour cream
- ½ cup shredded cheddar cheese
- 2 green onions (to be sliced, about ¼ cup)
- Favorite seasoning to taste

Instructions

1. Select the "Sauté" setting on the Instant Pot and the bacon when hot. Stir often as it cooks to crisp. Transfer the crisped bacon to a paper towel and discard the fat. Add the yellow onion, stirring occasionally for 2 minutes as it cooks. Add the garlic stir as it cooks for 30 seconds. Then press "Cancel" to stop sautéing. Add the potatoes and broth.
2. Securely lock the lid and turn the pressure release valve to "Sealing." Pressure cook on LE 6, (high pressure) for 6 minutes. When the timer beeps as it counts down to zero, use the quick release method. Then, carefully open the lid when all pressure is gone. Stir in the sour cream.

3. Using an immersion blender, puree the soup in the inner pot until the desired smoothness. Add the seasoning and serve with the cheese, bacon, and green onion as toppings. It can be topped with additional sour cream.

Yield: 6 servings.

Nutritional content per serving: Total fat: 7.8g, Carbs: 31.6g, Fiber: 2.5g, Protein: 9.1 g, Cholesterol 22mg, Calories: 232.

Chicken Noodle Soup

This Instant Pot Chicken Noodle Soup is another dimension to preparing a delicious, homey soup. It's easier than picking up a take-out. With just 5 ingredients, this warm, comfy soup is on your dining in about 30 minutes only. Veggies and noodles will cooperate to create the flavorful chicken broth in your the Instant Pot Duo Evo Plus.

Total cook time: 20 minutes.

Ingredients
- ½ lb. boneless skinless chicken breasts
- ½ cup carrot (to be peeled and chopped)
- 1 stalk celery (to be sliced, ½ cup)
- 2 oz. uncooked extra wide egg noodles (about 1 cup dry)
- 4 cups chicken broth
- Salt and pepper (to taste)

Instructions
1. Season the chicken with pepper and salt. Then add all the 5 ingredients in the Instant Pot. Lock the lid in place and turn the pressure release valve into the "Sealing" position. Choose the "Pressure Cook/Custom" function and select high pressure. Adjust the time to 5 minutes and press start. When the countdown reaches zero, quickly release the pressure.
2. Transfer the chicken to a tray and shred using two forks. Then return it to the pot and season to taste.
3. Serve and enjoy!

Yield: 4 servings.

Nutritional content per serving: Total fat: 1.2g, Carbs: 13.3g, Fiber: 1.3g, Protein: 11.8 g, Cholesterol 29mg, Calories: 120.

Tuscan Bean and Sausage Soup

This Instant Pot Tuscan Bean and Sausage Soup recipe is reminiscent of the wedding soup. But remember that you are in charge. So you could add chicken sausage instead of prepping meatballs. The inclusion of cannellini beans and kale results in extra satisfaction while chicken broth, garlic, and onion finish the flavor deal.

Total cook time: 30 minutes.

Ingredients

- 2 tbsp. olive oil
- ½ lb. Italian-style chicken sausage (casing removed)

- 1extra large onion (to be diced into about 1 ½ cups)
- 2 cloves garlic (to be minced)
- 1 can white cannellini beans (to be rinsed and drained, about 15 oz.)
- 1 tsp. Italian seasoning
- 4 cups chicken broth
- 3 cups packed finely-chopped kale leaves (leaves to be trimmed from stems before chopping)
- 2 tbsp. grated parmesan cheese

Instructions

1. Select the "Sauté" function on the Instant Pot and add the oil when hot. Add the sausage and cook until well browned, about 10 minutes. Stir often to separate meat. Stop sautéing by pressing "Cancel." Add the onion, garlic, seasoning, beans, and broth to the pot and mix well.
2. Lock the lid in place with the release valve turned to "Sealing." Select Pressure Cook/Custom and cook on High with the timer set to 3 minutes. Once the cook timer ends, quickly release the pressure.
3. Stir in the kale and leave for 5 minutes. Then season to taste and serve sprinkled with the cheese.

Yield: 6 servings.

Nutritional content per serving: Total fat: 6.9g, Carbs: 15.5g, Fiber: 3.0g, Protein: 13 g, Cholesterol 28mg, Calories: 181.

Creamy Instant Pot Chipotle Shrimp Soup

This creamy Instant Pot chipotle shrimp soup recipe is a fitting soup that comes perfect on the usual busy weekday. Loaded with potatoes, corn, bacon, and shrimp, it's finished with cream. The spicy kick comes from Chipotle chilies.

Total cook time: 30 minutes.

Ingredients

- 3 slices bacon (to be chopped)
- 1 cup diced onion
- ¾ cup chopped celery
- 1 tsp. garlic
- 1 tbsp. flour
- ¼ cup dry white wine
- 1 ½ cups chicken (or vegetable broth or seafood stock)
- ½ cup whole milk
- 1 ½ cups potatoes (cut into small 1/3-inch cubes)
- 1 cup frozen corn kernels
- 2 tsp. diced canned chipotle peppers in adobo sauce
- ¾ tsp. salt or to taste
- ½ tsp. black pepper
- ½ tsp. dried thyme
- ½ lb. shrimp peeled and deveined
- ¼ cup heavy cream

Instructions

1. Start the Instant Pot with the "Sauté" function. Add bacon to the inner pot and sauté for about 3 minutes or until crisp, stirring frequently. Add onions, celery, and garlic and continue sautéing for about 3 minutes more or until vegetables have softened. Add flour, stir and cook for less than 1 minute.
2. Press "Cancel" and then add white wine to deglaze the pot by scraping the brown bits off the bottom of the inner pot using a wooden spoon. If needed to completely deglaze, add 1 or 2 tablespoons of broth. Stir in broth, corn, milk, potatoes, Chipotle pepper, salt, black pepper, and thyme and mix well. Lock the lid in place and select the "Pressure Cook/Custom" function and cook for 1 minute. Then do a quick release of pressure.
3. Stir in shrimp, and then cream. Lock the Instant Pot again and leave to allow the residual heat to cook the shrimp for 10 minutes.
4. Serve garnished with scallions or any favorite garnishes.

Yield: 5 servings.

Nutritional content per serving: Total fat: 9g, Carbs: 38g, Fiber: 4g, Protein: 17 g, Cholesterol 84mg, Calories: 314.

CHAPTER 5: INSTANT POT DUO EVO PLUS BEANS & GRAIN

Beans have been known to be one of the richest sources of non-animal protein. Some in the beans family are perhaps the richest. You can do a whole lot with beans in their various species. So you've got the whole world to explore if you set your Instant pot Duo Evo Plus in motion to deal with your beans.

Grain, on the other hand, is stable in many lands. Thus, it will be a good meal in the Instant Pot too. Many of the popular grains are rich in protein and fiber. And they supply good amounts of carbs for your body.

Let's give attention to a few examples of simple beans and grains recipes in this chapter.

Quick Soak Dry Beans

Your beans can cook faster if you soak them. This can be a great alternative to canned beans. Thanks to the Instant Pot, cooking beans can be expedited and concluded in 30 minutes. Try out making the recipe here and use the resulting beans as a part of a bigger recipe.

Total cook time: 30 minutes.

Ingredients
- 2 cups dried beans
- Water (enough to cover the beans about 1-inch)

Instructions
1. After removing all foreign items from the beans, pour them into the inner pot of an Instant Pot. Add water to the beans. Securely close the lid with the steam release valve set to the "Sealing" position. Set the cook time to 5 minutes and pressure cook on high.
2. At the end of the cook time, do a Natural Pressure Release for 5 minutes and a quick release of the remaining pressure. When the pin drops, open the lid.
3. Discard the liquid and save the beans to be used in any recipe requiring soaked beans in the future.

Yield: Yield: 1 cup.
Nutritional content per serving: Total fat: 01.0g, Total Carbs: 40g, Protein: 15 g, Calories: 224, Dietary Fiber 13g.

Homemade Chili With Dried Beans

Dried beans and ground beef can make the chili that will be just the right comfort food for a wintry or fall evening. If you're expecting a crowd of visitors, this recipe can also be a great dish.

Total cook time: 1 hour 30 minutes.

Ingredients
- 1 ½ cups dried pinto beans (to be presoaked)

- 2 tbsp. vegetable oil
- 1 ½ lb. ground beef
- 2 cups onion (to be chopped)
- 1 cup bell pepper (to be chopped)
- 2 tbsp. minced garlic
- 3 tbsp. Mexican chili powder
- 1 tbsp. dried oregano
- 2 tsp. cumin powder
- 2 tsp. cocoa powder
- 1 tsp. salt (or to taste)
- ½ tsp. black pepper
- ¼ tsp. cayenne pepper (or to taste)
- 4 cups beef broth
- 1 can (14 oz.) diced tomatoes (or 2 cups fresh tomatoes, to be chopped)
- ¼ cup masa harina
- Any favorite topping

Instructions

1. Select the "Sauté" mode on the IP and add oil to the inner pot when hot. Add ground beef and stir with a wooden spatula for the meat to break up into smaller pieces. Continue sautéing for about 3 minutes or until meat is browned. Stir in onions and sauté about 2 minutes to soften. Add bell peppers and garlic and then, stir. Stir in the next 7 ingredients on the list one after the other. Leave for about 1 minute to fragrant and then, stir in the broth, tomatoes, and pre-soaked pinto beans.
2. Seal the lid in place, turning steam release valve to "Sealing". Set the time for 20 minutes and pressure cook on High Pressure. When the timer beeps, allow 15 minutes of natural pressure release and carefully open the pot once the pin drops.
3. Return the pot to the "Sauté" mode. Then, add masa harina and stir frequently for about 5 minutes or until thickened. Select "Cancel". Leave for 5 minutes to continue thickening.
4. Serve by ladling into serving bowls with your choice topping(s).

Yield: 8 servings.
Nutritional content per serving: Total fat: 13g, Carbs: 18g, Protein: 24g, Fiber 1g, Calories: 279.

Red Beans and Rice

The red species of beans, accompanied by rice, will make a popular meal at your next gathering. They may deceive, making visitors believe it's been cooked for hours. When saved for the next day, the taste becomes greater. The recipe is so simple and great for feeding a crowd.

Total cook time: 1 hour 20 minutes.
Ingredients

- 2 tbsp. vegetable oil
- 1 lb. andouille sausage (to be cut into slices)
- 1 cup onion (to be chopped)
- 1 cup bell pepper (to be chopped)
- 1 cup celery (to be chopped)
- 1 tbsp. garlic (to be minced)
- 1 tsp. dried thyme
- ½ tsp. cayenne pepper (or to taste)
- 1 tsp. (salt or to taste)
- 1 tsp. (black pepper or to taste)
- 4 cups (chicken broth or water)
- 2 bay leaves (large, or 3 small)
- 1 lb. small red beans (soaked overnight or quick-soaked, to be drained)
- 1 smoked ham hock (or ham shank)
- 4 green onions (to be chopped)
- ¼ cup parsley (to be chopped)
- 4 cups rice (cooked, to serve)
- Hot sauce (to serve as a side)

Instructions

1. Select the "Sauté" mode on the IP and add oil to the inner pot when hot. Add sausage and cook for 5-8 minutes or until browned. Use a slotted spoon to transfer the sausage to a medium bowl and then, set aside. Add the next 4 ingredients up to and including garlic to the pot and stir for 5 minutes or until onion is translucent. Add the next 4 ingredients up to black pepper and stir for about 30 seconds to coat. Add about half a cup of broth to the inner pot to deglaze by using a wooden spatula to scrape all brown bits from the bottom. Add the remaining broth together with bay leaves, ham hock, and red beans.
2. Tightly close the Instant Pot, turning the vent valve to "Sealing" and set time to 30 minutes. Pressure cook on high. When timer beeps, wait 20 minutes for a natural pressure release and carefully open the pot when the pin drops.
3. Transfer the ham hock into a tray and chop into bite-size pieces. Scoop out 1 cup of beans and mash with a fork. Return ham hock and mashed beans plus the reserved sausage to the pot. Stir well and then sauté for 5 minutes to allow the Instant Pot Red Beans to thicken.
4. Serve over rice with hot sauce as a side (optional). Garnish with parsley and green onions.

Yield: 8 servings.
Nutritional content per serving: Total fat: 22g, Carbs: 39g, Fiber: 5g, Protein: 18g, Calories: 421.

Sausage and White Bean–Stuffed Portobellos

If you doubt the saying that we eat with our eyes, try out this perfect dish and you will see the absolute beauty and scrumptious tastes with your very eyes! Any time or moment is cool to serve those portobellos as you will see in this recipe.

Total cook time: 38 minutes.

Ingredients

- 4 oz. sweet Italian turkey sausage (to be removed from casing)
- ½ cup no-salt-added tomato sauce
- 1 tbsp. dried basil
- ¼ tsp. crushed pepper flakes
- 4 oz. large portobello mushroom caps (to be wiped clean with a damp cloth)
- ½ can no-salt-added navy beans (to be rinsed and drained, 15 oz.)
- ¾ cup chopped red bell pepper
- 1 cup water
- 2 oz. fresh spinach (to be coarsely chopped)
- 4 oz. shredded mozzarella cheese (part-skim)
- 2 tbsp. grated parmesan cheese

Instructions

1. Press the "Sauté" button on the Instant Pot and adjust to a high setting. Add cooking spray to the pot when hot to coat. Add sausage and cook until it begins to brown on the edges, for 2 minutes. Stir frequently. Set aside in a bowl.
2. In a small bowl, add tomato sauce, dried basil, and crushed pepper flakes. Spoon equal amounts of tomato sauce on top of each mushroom with the gill side up. Top with equal amounts of beans, bell pepper, and sausage.
3. Add water to the pot and insert a steamer basket. Position the mushrooms in the steamer basket and allow it to overlap slightly, if necessary. Close the lid in place with the valve vent pointing to the "Sealing" position. Set to cook on Pressure Cook for 10 minutes. When the timer beeps, quick-release the pressure. Carefully remove the lid after the valve has dropped.
4. Top the mushrooms with the mozzarella and spinach. Put the lid on the pot without sealing for 5 minutes for the spinach to wilt. Sprinkle and serve with parmesan.

Yield: 4 servings.
Nutritional content per serving: Total fat: 8g, Total Carbs: 17g, Dietary Fiber: 5g, Protein: 18g, Cholesterol 35 mg, Calories: 210.

Three-Bean Vegetarian Chili

Beans love chili! It does wonder with the nutrition-packed vegetarian recipe that is low in fat. Don't feel restricted to three types of beans specified in this recipe. You can explore your cooking world with fun, taste, and visual appeal without feeling any guilt with any beans of your choice.

Total cook time: 50 minutes.

Ingredients

- 1 cup dried pinto beans (to be soaked overnight, covered, and drained)
- 1 cup dried red beans (to be soaked overnight, covered, and drained)
- 1 cup dried black beans (to be soaked overnight, covered, and drained)
- 2 medium white onions (to be peeled and chopped)
- 2 medium red bell peppers (to be seeded and chopped)
- 2 stalks celery (to be chopped)
- 1 can diced tomatoes (28 oz.)
- 1 can tomato sauce (15 oz.)
- ¼ cup chili powder
- 2 tbsp. smoked paprika
- 1 tsp. ground cumin
- 1 tsp. ground coriander
- ½ tsp. salt
- ½ tsp. ground black pepper
- 3 cups vegetable broth
- 1 cup water

Instructions

1. Combine all ingredients in the inner pot. Close the lid and set steam release to the "Sealing" position. Select the chili function with the default time of 30 minutes.
2. When the timer beeps, do a quick release of the pressure. When the pin has dropped, open the lid and stir the chili. For more thickness, press the "Cancel" and start the "Sauté" function to let the chili simmer. Leave uncovered until the desired thickness. Then, serve warm.

Yield: 8 servings.

Nutritional content per serving: Total fat: 2g, Total Carbs: 80g, Protein: 18g, Calories: 323.

Wheat Berry, Black Bean, and Avocado Salad

A wheat berry is a whole-wheat kernel comprising the edible portion of the whole wheat kernel without the shell. With black bean, the taste is great and good for an over-the-meal conversation with family or friends.

Total cook time: 55 minutes.

Ingredients

- 2 oz. dried black beans
- ½ cup hard wheat berries
- 4 cups water
- 1 container grape tomatoes (to be halved; 10 oz.)
- 1 cup chopped poblano chili peppers
- ½ cup chopped fresh cilantro
- 2 tbsp. cider vinegar
- 2 tbsp. extra-virgin olive oil
- 1 garlic clove minced
- ½ tsp. salt

- 1 avocado (to be peeled and chopped)
- ¾ cup shredded reduced-fat sharp cheddar cheese

Instructions

1. Add the beans and wheat berries together in a fine-mesh sieve. Rinse, drain, and pour into the Instant Pot with water. Seal the lid with the steam release valve on Sealing. Set the IP to cook on Pressure Cook for 25 minutes.
2. Meanwhile, combine the next 7 ingredients up to and including salt in a medium bowl and set aside.
3. When the timer beeps, use a quick pressure release and open when the pin has dropped. Carefully remove the lid. Drain the wheat berries and beans in a fine-mesh sieve. To cool quickly and stop the cooking process, run under cold water and drain well.
4. Add the drained bean mixture with avocado and cheese to the tomato mixture. Toss gently to coat and serve.

Yield: 4 servings.

Nutritional content per serving: Total fat: 17g, Total Carbs: 31g, Dietary Fiber: 9g, Protein: 13g, Cholesterol 15mg, Calories: 320.

Saucy Pinto Beans

When a bean dish is packed with bold flavors, they can be the perfect pick for a special or ordinary dinner night. You will have a wonderful satisfying taste. It can be served with brown rice and a side vegetable and make a complete meal.

Total cook time: 55 minutes.

Ingredients

- 2 cups (1 lb.) dry pinto beans
- 2 tbsp. avocado oil
- 1 large yellow onion (to be peeled and diced)
- 1 medium jalapeño (to be seeded and diced)
- 2 tsp. minced garlic
- 3 ½ cups chicken stock
- 8 oz. tomato sauce
- 2 tbsp. chili powder
- 1 tbsp. yellow mustard
- 1 tsp. dried oregano
- 1 tsp. cumin
- ½ tsp. black pepper
- 2 bay leaves
- ½ tsp. salt

Instructions

1. Soak the beans in a bowl covered with 3 inches of water for 4 to 8 hours.
2. Start the Instant Pot on the "Sauté" function and add oil when it displays the "Hot" message. After heating for about 1 minute, add the garlic, onion, and jalapeño. Sauté for about 5 minutes or until softened. Add the soaked beans, bay

leaves, chili powder, cumin, mustard, oregano, pepper, tomato sauce, and salt and stir well to combine. Add stock to deglaze by scraping any brown bits from the pot's bottom.

3. Firmly secure the lid with the vent valve on the "Sealing" position. Press the "Pressure Cook" button with the time adjusted to 25 minutes. When the timer beeps, allow about 15 minutes of natural pressure release until float valve drops. Carefully open the lid.

4. Remove the bay leaves and discard, and then transfer the beans to medium bowl for serving.

Yield: 8 servings.

Nutritional content per serving: Total fat: 5g, Total Carbs: 44g, Dietary Fiber: 10g, Protein: 16g, Calories: 289.

White Beans With Smoked Sausage

What about smoked sausage combining with white beans? You will get a budget-friendly bright aromatics, and tasty meal.

Total cook time: 2 hours.

Ingredients
- 2 tsp. olive oil
- 1 lb. smoked sausage (pork or turkey; to be cut into ½-inch disks)
- 1 small onion (to be finely chopped)
- 2 carrots (to be diced)
- 2 celery stalks (to be diced)
- 4 cups low-sodium chicken broth (to be warmed)
- 1 lb. dried small white beans (to be rinsed and picked over)
- 1 tbsp. chopped fresh thyme (or 1 tbsp. cajun seasoning)

Instructions
1. Start the Instant Pot on the "Sauté" function and add oil when it displays the "Hot" message. After heating for about 1 minute, brown the sausage on both sides and transfer to a shallow dish. Cover loosely with foil.

2. Sauté onion, carrots, and celery for 3-4 minutes or until onion is soft. Then deglaze the pot by adding broth and scraping using a wooden spoon to remove brown bits stuck to the bottom. Return the sausage into the pot and add sorted and rinsed beans. Stir to combine.

3. Select "Cancel" to turn off the pot. Firmly secure the lid with the vent release valve turned to "Sealing". Select the "Pressure Cook" function and turn the knob to set the time to 60 minutes. When the timer beeps, allow 15 minutes of natural pressure release. Then, do a then quick-release the remaining pressure.

4. Serve hot alongside fresh cornbread (optional).

Yield: 6 servings.

Green Beans With Mushrooms and Bacon

Cooking green beans has been made it easier and healthier than it used to be, thanks to the Instant pot Duo Evo Plus. Try out this recipe that includes mushrooms and just a few slices of bacon for a salty and smoky flavor.

Total cook time: 30 minutes.

Ingredients
- 4 bacon slices (to be chopped)
- 1 garlic clove (to be minced)
- 8 oz. button mushrooms (to be sliced)
- 1 cup low-sodium vegetable broth
- 1 lb. fresh or frozen green beans trimmed
- ½ medium lemon (to be juiced)
- 1 tbsp. balsamic vinegar

Instructions
1. Start the Instant Pot on the "Sauté" function for 2 minutes and add bacon, garlic, and mushrooms when it displays the "Hot" message. Continue sautéing until the bacon starts browning, about 6 minutes. Then cancel sautéing. Deglaze by adding the broth and using a wooden spoon to scrape up any browned bits from the bottom of the pot. Then, add green beans to the pot.
2. Firmly secure the lid into place and select "Pressure Cook" with the steam release set on the "Sealing" position. Set to cook on High and the time for 2 minutes. It can be up to 4 minutes if the green beans are frozen. When the timer beeps, do a quick release of the pressure and carefully unlock the lid to remove. Then, stir in the lemon juice and vinegar.
3. Serve immediately. You can also refrigerate for up to 3 days in an airtight container after cooling.

Yield: 6 servings.

Nutritional content per serving: Total fat: 6g, Total Carbs: 7g, Dietary Fiber: 3g, Protein: 8g, Calories: 104.

Sweet Potato & Black Bean Tacos

We beckon to Tacos! They're just what you need on any occasion. Delicious, filling, and moderately spicy, they're also nutritious—protein-packed and rich in vitamins A, B6, and C. What else can you expect from a combination of potatoes or beans? The combination is great for flour or corn tortillas.

Total cook time: 30 minutes.

Ingredients
- 1 tbsp. to olive oil
- ½ sweet onion (to be diced)
- 1 large sweet potato (to be diced)
- 1 red bell pepper (to be diced)
- 1 garlic clove (to be minced)
- 1 medium tomato (to be diced)
- 15 oz. black beans (1 can, to be rinsed and drained)

- 1 canned chipotle pepper adobo sauce (to be diced)
- 2 tsp. to adobo sauce from the can
- 2 tsp. chili powder
- ½ tsp. salt
- ½ tsp. ground cumin
- ½ cup homemade or store-bought vegetable stock
- 1 tbsp. freshly squeezed lime juice
- 1 lime zested
- Corn or flour tortillas (for serving)
- 1 avocado (to be peeled, pitted, and mashed)
- ¼ cup fresh cilantro (to be chopped)
- Garden salsa for serving (optional),
- Cashew sour cream for serving (optional)
- Jalapeño peppers for serving (optional, to be sliced)
- Red cabbage for serving (optional, to be sliced)

Instructions

1. Start the pot on the "Sauté" mode and once it displays the "Hot" message, add the oil. Heat for about 2 minutes and add onion when it shimmers. Sauté and stir for 1 minute. Add the potato and bell pepper and cook for another 1 minute while you keep stirring to avoid burning anything. Then, cancel sautéing and add the garlic. Cook and stir often for about 30 seconds.
2. Add the adobo sauce, black beans, chili powder, chipotle, cumin, tomato, and, salt. Add the lime juice and stock. Firmly lock the lid and have the steam release turned to the "Sealing". Select the "Pressure Cook" function and set to cook on high for 4 minutes.
3. When the timer beeps, wait for 5 minutes to let the pressure release naturally. Then quick-release any remaining pressure. Remove the lid once the pin drops. You may sauté for 1-2 minutes more if there is too much liquid in the inner pot, while you constantly stir.
4. Stir in the lime zest and serve in the tortillas topped with mashed avocado and cilantro.

Yield: 5 servings.

Nutritional content per serving: Total fat: 16g, Total carbs: 51g, Dietary Fiber: 15g, Protein: 12 g, Cholesterol 84mg, Calories: 369.

CHAPTER 6: INSTANT POT DUO EVO PLUS
BEEF, PORK & LAMB

Nothing cooks better in the Instant Pot Duo Evo Plus than meat! Is that an overstatement? Beef, pork, and lamb are the commonest meats besides seafood and foods in feathers. The rich source of animal protein is the next on the list of recipes in this Instant Pot cookbook.

There's hardly an end to what can be done with beef, pork, and lamb. In this chapter, you will come across how experienced chefs have masterfully made stroganoffs, goulash, and even lasagna with a combination of potatoes and other supports and sides.

Pork and lamb also have come to the party. Pull pork and the one with beer roots are marking their presence on the roll call. The same is with the decent appearance of lamb meats ably represented by the korma.

Easy Beef Stroganoff

Taking this Easy Beef Stroganoff recipe through the Instant Pot Duo Evo Plus, everything, including the egg noodles, cooks just right. The cream of mushroom soup and sour cream gives the classic flavor of a stroganoff. Note that the cook time has been cut down in this recipe by using beef sirloin.

Total cook time: 60 minutes.

Ingredients
- 1 large onion (to be diced into about 1 cup)
- 1 ¼ lb. boneless beef sirloin steak (to be cut into thin strips)
- 1 tsp. paprika
- ½ tsp. garlic powder
- 4 cups extra-wide uncooked egg noodles
- 2 cups water (or beef broth)
- 2 tsp. Worcestershire sauce
- 1 can (10 ½ oz.) condensed cream of mushroom soup (Campbell's is recommended)
- ¼ cup sour cream
- 2 tbsp. chopped fresh parsley

Instructions
1. Season the beef steak with salt and pepper in the inner pot. Layer on the beef the onion, paprika, powder, and noodles in the pot. Add the broth and sauce over the noodles and spoon (without stirring) the soup on top.
2. Lock the lid securely and set the pressure release valve to the "Sealing" position. Select "Pressure Cook" and set to cook on high pressure with the timer set to 8 minutes. When the timer counts down to zero, release the pressure with the quick-release method.
3. Gradually stir in the sour cream leave for 5 minutes uncovered. Before serving, season to taste and sprinkle with parsley.

Yield: Yield: 6 servings.
Nutritional content per serving: Total Fat: 9.5 g, Total Carbs: 25.8g, Protein: 26.3 g, Dietary Fiber: 1.8g, Calories: 300, Cholesterol: 67mg.

Ground Beef and Noodle Goulash

This dish is more like a casserole glorifying the goodness of paprika. With a lot of peppery flavors that aren't just a red coloring agent, you don't have to use the usual use "hot" Hungarian paprika. But as you have a better bottling of ground paprika, you may make all the difference.

Total cook time: 45 minutes.

Ingredients
- 3 ½ cups diced tomatoes (packed in juice in 28-oz. can)
- 2 cups beef (or chicken) broth
- 2 whole jarred red peppers (to be roasted and cut into thin strips)
- 1 tbsp. mild paprika
- 2 tsp. stemmed and minced fresh oregano leaves (or 1 tsp. dried oregano)
- ½ tsp. fennel seeds
- ½ tsp. table salt
- 1 lb. frozen ground beef
- 12 oz. regular dried egg noodles

Instructions
1. Add the first seven ingredients on the list, up to and including salt, one after the other, to the inner pot, stirring each time. Gently add the chunk of ground beef into the sauce. Tightly lock the lid onto the pot with the vent valve closed. Select the Pressure Cook function and set to cook on high pressure for 15 minutes. When the timer beeps signifying the end of cook time, do a quick release of pressure to release the remaining pressure.
2. Carefully and open the cooker. Using a large metal spoon and a fork, break the ground beef chunk into bite-sized small bits to look like tiny pink or red meatballs. Stir in the noodles and return the lid to cover the pot. Then lock as usual and select the Pressure Cook setting again with the cook time set to 4 minutes this time, cook on high.
3. Again, when the timer beeps, quick-release the pressure let the steam spew out completely. When the pin drops, carefully open the pot.
4. Stir well and then serve.

Yield: 6 servings.
Nutritional content per serving: Total Fat: 13 g, Total Carbs: 18g, Protein: 24g, Dietary Fiber: 3g, Calories: 279, Cholesterol: 53mg.

All-American Pot Roast

This pot roast is like a road map as you can customize the root vegetables to suit your taste. They just have to be fairly large, like 2-inch chunks so they don't turn to mush as they cook evenly. This recipe calls for plenty of Worcestershire sauce for more flavor.

Total cook time: 1 hour 20 minutes.

Ingredients
- 1 ½ cups beef broth
- ½ cup frozen chopped onion (or 1 small yellow or white onion, to be peeled and chopped)
- 1 tbsp. Worcestershire sauce
- 2 tsp. peeled and minced garlic
- 1 frozen (3-3 ½ lb.) boneless beef chuck roast
- 1 tsp. mild paprika
- 1 tsp. onion powder
- 1 tsp. dried thyme
- ½ tsp ground black pepper
- 2 lb. peeled root vegetables (taken from carrots, potatoes, rutabaga, sweet potatoes, turnips, butternut squash or any winter squash, to be cut into 2-inch chunks and seeded as necessary)

Instructions
1. Combine the broth, onion, Worcestershire sauce with garlic in an Instant Pot. Set the pot rack or a large open vegetable steamer inside the pot. Set the chuck roast on the rack (or in the steamer) and sprinkle the top evenly with onion powder, paprika, thyme, and pepper. Securely lock the lid onto the pot with the steam release valve pointing to the "Sealing" position.
2. Select "Pressure Cook" on high with the timer set to 1 hour 20 minutes. Once the timer beeps, use the quick-release method to let the steam out. Then, carefully remove the lid and open the cooker. Using kitchen tongs or silicone cooking mitts, remove the rack or steamer from the cooker and allow the chuck roast into the sauce inside. Distribute the root vegetables over the mixture and lock the lid back onto the pot.
3. Select "Pressure Cook" and turn the knob to select 10 minutes cooking on high pressure. Remember to set the valve to the "Sealing" position. When the timer beeps, allow 30 minutes of natural pressure release and carefully open when the pin has dropped.
4. Use a large slotted spoon or large metal spatula with a fork, move the chuck roast to a cutting board and leave there to cool for about 5 minutes. Slice the meat into chunks and serve with the vegetables and the resulting sauce from the pot.

Yield: 6 servings.

Nutritional content per serving: Total fat: 22g, Total Carbs: 39g, Dietary Fiber: 5g, Protein: 18 g, Calories: 421, Cholesterol: 35mg.

Lazy Lasagna

Making Lazy Lasagna doesn't make you lazy. But the recipe comes together fast and easy in the Instant Pot. That's all and it'll be your family's delight.

Total cook time: 38 minutes.

Ingredients
- 1 tbsp. olive oil
- 1 tbsp. butter
- 1 small onion (to be chopped)

- 1 tbsp. minced garlic
- 2 lb. lean ground beef
- 1 jar pasta sauce
- 2 cups beef broth
- ¼ cup red wine
- 1 cup water
- 1 tbsp. Italian seasoning
- 8 oz. uncooked lasagna noodles (or other pasta)
- 2 cups shredded mozzarella cheese (to be divided)
- ¼ cup Parmesan cheese
- 1 cup ricotta cheese

Instructions

1. Start the Instant Pot on the "Sauté" mode and add the olive oil and butter when hot. Allow it to sizzle and add onions and garlic cook. Continue sautéing for 2 minutes. Stir it regularly.
2. Add ground beef and cook for about 5 minutes or until the pinkness is all gone. Drain the grease and return the beef the pot. Add pasta sauce, broth, wine, water, and seasonings. Stir well to combine. Add pasta and stir to ensure that the liquid covers noodles.
3. Select the Pressure Cook option on the Instant Pot and set to cook on high for 20 minutes. Lock the lid in place and have the steam release valve turned to Sealing. When the cook time ends, wait for natural release pressure and carefully open the lid when the pressure is completely gone.
4. Add cheese and stir gently. You may reserve about ½ cup mozzarella cheese for a sprinkle if you would like a bit of it on top of the lasagna while serving.

Yield: 4 servings.

Nutritional content per serving: Total fat: 8.0g, Total Carbs: 17g, Dietary Fiber: 5g, Protein: 18g, Cholesterol 35 mg, Calories: 201.

Beefy Potato Au Gratin

This recipe is about chili packed with nutrition. You can enjoy it without a guilty feeling because it is low in fat. Yet, it will give you that full feeling for such a long time. The spice mixture recipes here are just a sample of coordination. So you are free to tinker with it.

Total cook time: 40 minutes.

Ingredients
For spice mixture:
- 1 tbsp. Italian seasoning
- 2 tsp. paprika
- 1 tsp. salt
- ¼ tsp. pepper
- ¼ tsp. rosemary (to be crushed)

Beefy Potato Au Gratin:
- 1 lb. ground beef (preferably 93% lean)
- 1 tsp. kosher salt
- ¼ tsp. pepper

- ½ + ¾ cup beef (or chicken) broth
- 2 ½ lb. russet potatoes (to be cut into ¼-inch slices)
- 1 ½ cups shredded cheddar
- Chopped fresh parsley (optional, for garnish)

Instructions

1. Combine the spice mixture ingredients in a small bowl and mix thoroughly.
2. Select the "Sauté" function on the Instant Pot and add the ground beef. Sauté and stir until all pink disappears. Then transfer the beef browned meat to a dish. Cover loosely with foil.
3. Rinse the pot with water and start sautéing again. Coat with nonstick spray and add ½ cup of broth in the pot. Also, add 1/3 of the potatoes, 1/3 of the beef, 1/3 of the cheese, and 1/3 of the spice mixture in that order.
4. Divide the remaining potatoes, cheeses, beef, and spice mixture into two and layer each part as done earlier. Pour ¾ cup of broth on the pot and cover. Tightly secure it and ensure that the vent valve is in the "Sealing" position. Then select the "Pressure Cook" function and set the time to 15 minutes.
5. Immediately the timer beeps, use the quick release of the pressure and carefully open. Then serve hot.

Yield: 6 servings.

Nutritional content per serving: Total fat: 2g, Carbs: 60g, Dietary Fiber: 17 g, Protein: 18 g, Calories:323.

Texas Beef Brisket

You don't have to get Texas before you enjoy these cuts of meat. The recipe allows the use of a variety of spice if you can have a nice blend of them. With 8 hours of refrigerating, you can expect a kind of special barbecue as the meat would have absorbed enough spice.

Total cook time: 55 minutes.

Ingredients
For spice mixture:
- 3 tbsp. smoked paprika
- 3 tbsp. brown sugar
- 2 tbsp. kosher salt
- 1 ½ tbsp. onion powder
- 1 ½ tbsp. garlic powder
- 2 tsp. pepper
- 1 ½ tsp. ground cumin
- 1 tsp. chipotle chili powder
- 1 tsp. dried oregano leaves
- ¾ tsp. ground mustard
- ½ tsp. cayenne pepper (optional)

For Texas Beef Brisket:
- 4-5 lb. beef brisket (fat trimmed to ¼-inch or less, cut into two pieces)
- 1 cup water
- ½ cup BBQ sauce

Instructions
1. In a bowl, combine the spice mixture ingredients and rub on the trimmed brisket. Place brisket in a ziplock bag or other airtight container. Refrigerate for 8 hours or overnight.
2. When ready to cook, pour water in the inner pot and insert the steam rack. Position the brisket pieces on the rack with the fat side up. Tightly cover the pot with the steam release valve pointing to Sealing. Select the Pressure Cook function and set the time to 75 minutes. When the timer beeps, allow 15 minutes of natural pressure release. Then do a quick release of the remaining pressure.
3. Carefully transfer the meat to a baking sheet covered with foil. Brush with BBQ sauce. Bring the brisket to broil for 4-5 minutes. When it's caramelized and bubbly, slice and serve.

Yield: 4 servings.
Nutritional content per serving: Total fat: 17g, Total Carbs: 31g, Dietary Fiber: 9g, Protein: 13 g, Cholesterol 15 mg, Calories: 320.

Lamb Korma

Korma is a kind of meat served from generation to generation in restaurants. But you don't need to make the journey the 100-year-old restaurant to enjoy your Lamb Korma. You can make it right in your home by following this recipe and uniquely enjoy your lamb.

Total cook time: 1 hour.

Ingredients
- 1 cup plain yogurt
- ½ cup garlic (to be minced)
- 2 tbsp. ginger (to be minced)
- 2 tbsp. amchur powder
- 1 tbsp. ground cumin
- ½ tsp. ground cloves
- 1 tbsp. freshly ground black pepper
- 1 tbsp. kosher salt
- 2 tsp. Kashmiri chili powder
- 1 ½ lb. lamb stewing meat (to be cut into 2-inch pieces)
- 3 tbsp. vegetable oil
- 8 green cardamom pods (to be cracked)
- 3 cinnamon sticks (2-inch)
- 1 cup low-sodium beef broth
- ½ cup chopped cilantro
- ½ cup store-bought crispy fried onions

Instructions
1. Whisk together the first 9 ingredients on the list in a large bowl. Add the meat to the mixture and stir to let the meat be evenly coated by the mixture. Place brisket in a ziplock bag or other airtight container. Refrigerate for 8 hours or overnight.
2. When ready to cook, start the Instant Pot on the Sauté function and add oil to the hot pot and then, sauté for about 1 minute or until shimmering. Add the cracked cardamom pods and cinnamon and cook for 1 minute or until fragrant. Add the

marinated lamb and stir in the broth. Cover and lock the lid in place and pressure cook on LE 6 for 23 minutes.

3. When the timer beeps, wait for 10 minutes of natural pressure release and then carefully release the remaining pressure. Add cilantro and more salt, (if needed).
4. Serve with crispy fried onion as a garnish.

Yield: 4 servings.

Nutritional content per serving: Total fat: 5g, Total Carbs: 44g, Dietary Fiber: 10g, Protein: 16 g, Calories: 289.

Simple Tasty Pulled Pork

Turning attention back to pork, we have this simple pulled pork to look to. With only a few ingredients, this recipe takes just 5 minutes or thereabouts to pull together. Let us find out it will happen with just pork loin with a few other ingredients locked inside the Instant Pot.

Total cook time: 1 hour 10 minutes.

Ingredients
- 1 extra-large onion (to be cut in half and sliced into about 1 ½ cups)
- 1 ½ lb. boneless pork loin (to be cut in half lengthwise)
- 2 tbsp. packed light brown sugar
- 2 tsp. chili powder
- 1 can roasted red pepper cooking soup (Campbell's is recommended, 10 ½ oz.)
- 2 tbsp. cider vinegar
- 4 soft white hamburger buns (the one from Pepperidge Farm recommended to be toasted)

Instructions
1. Layer the onion into the inner pot. Season the pork with salt and pepper and sprinkle with brown sugar and chili powder. Set the pork in the Instant Pot. Meanwhile, in a small bowl, stir the soup and vinegar to make a soup mixture and pour over the pork.
2. Securely lock the lid with the steam release valve pointing to the sealing position. Select the Pressure Cook function and set the time to 40 minutes. When the timer counts down to zero, carefully turn the valve to venting for a quick release of pressure.
3. Transfer the pork to a cutting board and select the Sauté setting. Continue sautéing the sauce mixture for about 5 minutes to thicken. Meanwhile, shred the pork. Then return the shredded pork to the pot to mix with the sauce. Season to taste and serve the mixture on the buns.

Yield: 6 servings.

Nutritional content per serving: Total fat: 8.2g, Total Carbs: 32.7g, Dietary Fiber: 3.2 g, Protein: 39.7 g, Cholesterol 91mg, Calories: 365.

Root Beer Pulled Pork

Let's see another way to try our culinary skills on the pulled pork. What makes the difference here is the root ingredient—the root beer and a little tinkering with the instructions.

Total cook time: 1 hour 20 minutes.

Ingredients
- 1 bone-in pork shoulder roast (visible to be fat removed, 3- 4 lb.)
- 2 tbsp. vegetable oil
- 1 tsp. salt
- ½ cup good quality regular root beer
- 1 cup barbecue sauce of choice (to be divided)

Instructions
1. Start the Instant Pot on the normal Sauté mode and add oil when hot. Allow it to simmer for 1- 2 minutes. Cut roast into 2 and add to the pot. Allow it cook for about 3 minutes each side or until browned. Press Cancel to stop sautéing.
2. Meanwhile, whisk together salt, root beer, and a half cup of barbecue sauce and pour the mixture evenly over the roast. Cover the pot and seal the lid into place with the steam release valve pointing to the "Sealing" position. Select "Pressure Cook" and program to cook on high for 45 minutes. When the cook time is up, wait for 10 minutes of the natural release of part of the pressure and quick-release the remaining pressure. Transfer the meat to a large cutting board; let cool to warm.
3. In the meantime, start the pot on sauté and simmer the juices for about 12 minutes. Whisk frequently as it cooks until it thickens and reduces to about 1 cup of sauce. Stir the remaining barbecue sauce into the pot. Shred and return the meat to the pot. Toss everything and until coated with the sauce. Then serve on buns or enjoy as the main dish.

Yield: 6-8 servings.

Nutritional content per serving: Total fat: 6g, Total Carbs: 7g, Dietary Fiber: 3g, Protein: 8g, Calories: 104.

Chipotle-Pork Tacos

Tacos can be made from anything. Chipotle pork is no exemption. This simple recipe makes tacos from the pork loin and it's simply delicious.

Total cook time: 1 hour.

Ingredients
- 1 tsp. oil
- 1 ½ lb. pork loin (to be cut into 1 ½-inch pieces)
- ½ cup water
- 1 jar Instant Pot Smoky Chipotle Sauce (15 oz.)

Instructions
1. Start the Instant Pot on the high Sauté mode and add oil when hot. Add meat and cook 5 minutes, stirring frequently.
2. Add water and sauce but don't stir. Close and lock the lid into place with the steam release valve turned to "Sealing". Select the Pressure Cook option and set to cook on high pressure. When the timer counts down to zero, carefully do a quick release of pressure. When the pin drops, carefully open the pot and serve.

Yield: 5 servings.

Nutritional content per serving: Total fat: 16g, Total Carbs: 51g, Dietary Fiber: 15g, Protein: 12 g, Calories: 369.

CHAPTER 7: INSTANT POT DUO EVO PLUS FISH/SEAFOOD RECIPES

Fish is not the only food that resides in the sea. But it is the most popular and commonest in the dishes. That's why this chapter is not limited to the discussion of just fishes. The sea is teeming with nutritious and healthy foods just too numerous to be counted.

However, how delicious these will be on the table will depend to a large extent on the skills of those who are in charge of the cooking. One thing is sure in all cases; the Instant Pot Duo Evo Plus can enhance whatever is brought to the table. Soups, stews, and sauces made with seafood, for instance, tastes a lot better than the ones in other pots.

Check out examples of such recipes in this chapter.

Steamed Fish with Greens and Miso Butter

Miso soup is the common name that has almost taken the shine out of the miso itself. But miso is not just about soup. This fermented soybean paste can also be condiment miso butter as you can see in this recipe that fields it alongside fish with aromatic greens.

Total cook time: 25 minutes.

Ingredients
- 1 cup vegetable (or chicken) broth
- 1-inch piece fresh ginger (to be peeled and cut into matchsticks)
- 1 clove garlic (to be sliced)
- 2 white fish fillets (such as tilapia, about 12 oz. in total)
- 1 tsp. soy sauce
- Salt and pepper to taste
- 1 tbsp. butter (at room temperature)
- 1 ½ tsp. miso paste
- ¼ lemon
- 1 bunch kale (tough stems to be removed and leaves to be torn, about 4 packed cups)

Instructions
1. Pour the broth to the Instant pot and add ginger and garlic. Place the trivet in the inner pot followed by a piece of aluminum foil. Position the fish fillets on top of the foil, side by side and drizzle with soy sauce. Season with salt and pepper. Tightly close the lid, with steam release valve pointing to Sealing. Pressure cook at low pressure for 8 to 9 minutes depending on the fillets' thickness.
2. Meanwhile, prepare your miso butter by mixing the butter and miso very well in a small bowl. Then set aside.
3. When the cook time is up, use the quick release method to let out the pressure and once all the pressure is released, carefully remove the fish using the foil after first checking for its doneness. Top with a squeeze of lemon juice.
4. Use a kitchen mitt to remove the trivet. Then start the Sauté function and add the kale once the pot simmers. Cook for about 2 minutes or until wilted. Turn off the

Sauté function. Use the tongs or a slotted spoon to remove it and season with salt and pepper.
5. Serve the greens with miso butter while topping with the fish fillets.

Yield: Yield: 3 servings.

Nutritional content per serving: Total fat: 9.5 g, Total Carbs: 25.8 g, Protein: 26.3 g, Dietary Fiber 1.8 g Calories: 300, Cholesterol 67 mg.

Fish Taco Bowls

Starting with fish, we proceed to this spicy taco bowl. Taco again! Yes, this time it is producing something handy as meal prep or something that can be used to spice dinner meals up. The smoky chili powder flavor in the fish goes along well with a creamy slaw. The jalapenos can be substituted or omitted.

Total cook time: 25 minutes.

Ingredients
- 4 cups shredded cabbage
- ¼ cup mayo
- 2 tbsp. sour cream
- 1 lime (to be halved)
- 2 tbsp. pickled jalapenos (to be chopped)
- 3 tilapia fillets (4 oz.)
- 2 tsp. chili powder
- 1 tsp. cumin
- 1 tsp. garlic powder
- 1 tsp. salt
- 2 tbsp. coconut oil
- 1 avocado (to be diced)
- 4 tbsp. fresh chopped cilantro

Instructions
1. Combine cabbage, mayo, sour cream, half of the lime juice, and jalapenos in a large bowl. Cover and refrigerate for at least 30 minutes before serving.
2. Start the pot on the Sauté mode. Pat fillets dry and sprinkle with seasonings. Add coconut oil and continue sautéing. Add tilapia and sear each side for 2-4 minutes, or until fully cooked and flakes easily. Press the Cancel button.
3. Chop the fish into bite-sized pieces. Separate the slaw into four bowls and place the fish on top.
4. Divide avocado among bowls and squeeze the other half of lime juice over each dish and then, sprinkle with cilantro.

Yield: 4 servings.

Nutritional content per serving: Total fat: 13 g, Total Carbs: 18 g, Protein: 24 g, Dietary Fiber 3 g Calories: 279, Cholesterol 53 mg.

Cod Chowder

This fish recipe is about chowder. Potatoes and corn will use the clam juice as their milk to give this cod a befitting taste at the party. Once again, you can alter the ingredients by substituting with other favorites.

Total cook time: 30 minutes.

Ingredients
- 2 tbsp. vegetable oil
- 1 lb. unpeeled red potatoes (to be diced)
- 2 medium leeks (to be halved and thinly sliced)
- 2 stalks celery (to be diced)
- 1 bulb fennel (to be diced)
- ½ tsp. yellow or red bell pepper (to be diced)
- 2 tsp. chopped fresh thyme
- 1 ¼ tsp. salt
- ½ tsp. black pepper
- 2 tbsp. all-purpose flour
- 2 cups clam juice
- 1 cup water
- 1 ½ lb. cod cut into 1-inch pieces
- 1 cup frozen corn
- 1 cup half and half
- ¼ cup fresh Italian parsley (to be finely chopped)

Instructions
1. Start the pot by selecting the Sauté function. Add oil when the message "Hot" displays and heat to simmer. Then, add the next 8 ingredients as listed on the recipe list. Cook for about 8 minutes for the vegetables to be slightly softened. Stir occasionally. Stir in the flour and allow it to cook for 1 minute. Add clam juice and water and mix well.
2. Firmly secure the lid with steam release valve turned to the Sealing position. Select Pressure Cook and program for 6 minutes at high pressure.
3. When the timer counts down to zero, do a quick release of the pressure. Insert an immersion blender to puree the soup until slightly thickened but not to complete smoothness.
4. Return the pot to the Sauté function and add cod, corn, half-and-half, and parsley. Cook stirring occasionally until soup starts simmering and fish firms and opaque, about 2 minutes. Then serve.

Yield: 6 servings.

Nutritional content per serving: Total fat: 22 g, Total Carbs: 39 g, Protein: 18 g, Dietary Fiber 5 g, Calories: 421, Cholesterol 35 mg.

Salmon and Vegetables With Lemon-Butter Sauce

This recipe is an example of show-stopping dishes which are actually very simple to make. With or without planning, just grab salmon fillets and start cooking right away along with red potatoes and carrots. Coat everything with the butter sauce produce for a flavorful, healthy meal.

Total cook time: 30 minutes.

Ingredients

- 1 cup low-sodium vegetable broth
- 2 lb. medium red potatoes (to be cut into 1-inch chunks)
- 4 pieces carrots (to be peeled and chopped into 1-inch thick, about 2 cups)
- 5 frozen salmon fillets (4 oz. each)
- 4 tbsp. unsalted butter (to be melted)
- ½ tsp. garlic powder
- 2 lemons (to be juiced)
- Freshly ground black pepper
- Fresh chopped dill (optional, for garnish)
- 1 tsp. fine sea salt (or to taste)

Instructions

1. Pour the broth into the pot and add potatoes and carrots. Place the fillets on top of the vegetables, skin-side down. Pour the melted butter and sprinkle with salt and garlic powder.
2. Secure the lid into place and ensure that the steam release knob turns to the sealed position. Then, select the Pressure Cook program to cook for 5 minutes on high pressure. When the timer counts down to zero, wait 10 minutes for a naturally release pressure. Then quick-release any remaining pressure. Carefully unlock to remove the lid.
3. Serve the salmon immediately garnished with black pepper and dill. You can, alternatively, store the salmon and vegetables in a ziplock bag or an airtight container to be refrigerated for up to 4 days.

Yield: 5 servings.

Nutritional content per serving: Total fat: 14 g, Total Carbs: 34 g, Protein: 27 g, Dietary Fiber 4 g Calories: 362.

Salmon With Red Potatoes and Spinach

One of the amazing beauties of the Instant Pot Duo Evo Plus is that you'll be able to cook your entire dinner in one pot. This is exemplified in the salmon with red garlicky potatoes and spinach. It will make your family dinner just right.

Total cook time: 25 minutes.

Ingredients

- 1 lb. small red potatoes (to be quartered)
- 1 cup water
- 1 ¼ tsp. salt (to be divided)
- ¾ tsp. black pepper (to be divided)
- 4 salmon filets (5 oz. each)
- ¼ tsp. sweet paprika
- ½ tsp. lemon zest
- 4 garlic cloves (to be minced)
- 2 tbsp. avocado oil
- 4 cups packed baby spinach
- 4 lemon wedges

Instructions

1. With the potatoes in the inner pot, add 1 cup of water, ¼ teaspoon of salt, and ¼ teaspoon of pepper. Set a steam rack on the potatoes.
2. Top the salmon with the paprika, lemon zest, ½ teaspoon of salt, and ¼ teaspoon of pepper. Set the salmon on the steam rack.
3. Firmly secure the lid with the steam release valve pointing to Sealing. Press Pressure Cook button program to cook for 3 minutes. When the timer beeps, allow the natural release of pressure and wait until float valve drops. Unlock the lid and open.
4. Take the salmon out of the steam rack and set aside. Select the Sauté function and cook the potatoes for about 30 seconds. Add the garlic and cook for an additional 90 seconds, stirring frequently. Stir in the oil and the remaining pepper and salt. Using a fork, gently mash the potatoes to the desired chunky texture. And press Cancel to stop sautéing.
5. Add the spinach and stir well for about 2, or until wilted. Serve with spinach and lemon wedges.

Yield: 4 servings.

Nutritional content per serving: Total fat: 11 g, Total Carbs: 20 g, Protein: 32 g, Dietary Fiber 3 g Calories: 332.

Halibut With Pineapple Avocado Salsa

Although halibut has such a simple taste, treating it with a creamy, sweet and spicy salsa such as from pineapple and avocado will bring out a flavorful and beautiful taste. Pineapple salsa is important in this recipe for its anti-inflammatory properties. This makes a great dinner with either rice or quinoa.

Total cook time: 20 minutes.

Ingredients
- 2 medium avocados (to be peeled, pitted, and diced)
- 1 cup diced pineapple
- 2 medium tomatoes (to be seeded and diced)
- 1 medium jalapeño pepper (to be seeded and diced)
- ½ cup chopped cilantro
- 1 medium lime (to be juiced)
- 1 tsp. salt (to be divided)
- 1/8 tsp. cayenne pepper
- 4 halibut fillets (4 oz. each)
- ¼ tsp. black pepper
- 1 cup water

Instructions
1. In a medium bowl, combine the first 6 ingredients on the list with a half teaspoon of salt and cayenne pepper; refrigerate. Meanwhile, sauté the halibut seasoned with the remaining half teaspoon of salt and black pepper.
2. Pour water in the inner pot and position the steam rack in it. Place the halibut on the steam rack. Tightly secure the lid with the steam release valve pointing to the "Sealing" position. Select the Pressure Cook/Custom function and program to cook

for 3 minutes. When the timer counts down to zero, allow about 3 minutes of natural pressure release until float valve drops. Then unlock the lid.
3. Serve the halibut filets topping each filet with a part of pineapple avocado salsa.
Yield: 4 servings.
Nutritional content per serving: Total fat: 11 g, Total Carbs: 14 g, Dietary Fiber: 6 g, Protein: 23 g, Calories: 250.

Tilapia With Pineapple Salsa

Let's try something else with pineapple salsa. This time, it is tilapia cooked in a foil packet. It will always come out moist and tender if you got it right. Tilapia plus pineapple salsa is always a wonderful flavor.

Total cook time: 20 minutes.

Ingredients
- 1 lb. tilapia fillets
- ¼ tsp. salt
- 1/8 tsp. black pepper
- 1 cup water
- ½ cup pineapple salsa

Instructions
1. Set the tilapia in the center of 1 ½-inch piece foil and season with salt and pepper. Make a bowl of the foil by folding it up on all sides and then pour in salsa. Also, fold the foil over the top of tilapia and then crimp edges.
2. Lower the trivet into the Instant Pot and set the foil packet on the trivet. Tightly close the lid and have the steam release valve set to Sealing. Select the Pressure Cook function and adjust the time to 2 minutes. When the timer counts down to zero, do a quick release of pressure and then unlock lid to remove it.
3. Take the foil packet out of the Instant Pot and open it. The steam will naturally release from inside. Then serve tilapia, garnish with salsa.
Yield: 4 servings.
Nutritional content per serving: Total fat: 2 g, Total Carbs: 3 g, Dietary Fiber: 1 g, Protein: 23 g, Calories: 124.

Simple Steamed Salmon Filets

With the help of a steam rack, you can avoid the common issue surrounding overcooking filets. If you steam them, you can avoid having them sit on the water and thereby breaking apart. You need to adjust the timing based on the thickness of the salmon fillets.

Total cook time: 10 minutes.

Ingredients
- 1 cup water (or any brand of dry white wine)
- 2 frozen skin-on salmon filets (6 oz. each)
- 4 paper-thin fresh lemon slices (to be seeded)
- ½ tsp. ground black pepper
- ¼ tsp. table salt

Instructions

1. With water or white wine in the Instant Pot, set the pot's rack (handles up) or a large open vegetable steamer in position inside the pot. The filets should be skin-side down, arranged such that they slightly overlap (avoid stacking them). Set two slightly overlapping lemon slices on each salmon filet. Evenly sprinkle the fish and lemon slices with salt and pepper. Lock the lid into place and set the steam release valve on the Sealing position.
2. Use the Meat/Stew or Pressure Cook setting and cook on high pressure for 6 minutes. Immediately the timer beeps, do a quick release of the pressure. Carefully unlatch to open. Using a metal spatula, transfer the fillets into serving plates.

Yield: 2 servings.

Nutritional content per serving: Total fat: 8.2 g, Total Carbs: 32.7 g, Dietary Fiber: 3.2 g, Protein: 39.7 g, Cholesterol 91 mg, Calories: 365.

Southwestern Shrimp Soup

Shrimps soups taste a lot like its toppings and servings. The ingredients in this recipe are divided into three so that all can see the area each item is needed.

Total cook time: 1 hour 20 minutes.

Ingredients
For topping:
- ½ cup sour cream
- 1 tsp. ground cumin
- ½ tsp. kosher salt

For pot:
- 1 tbsp. olive oil
- 2 cloves garlic (to be minced)
- 14 ½ oz. diced tomatoes (1 can, undrained)
- 15 ½ oz. white hominy with liquid (1 can, drained)
- 1 tsp. kosher salt
- ¼ tsp. black pepper
- 1 lb. medium shrimp (to be peeled, deveined, and frozen)
- Hot sauce (Chipotle Tabasco recommended)

For serving:
- ½ cup fresh cilantro leaves (optional)
- 1 lime (to be quartered)

Instructions

1. In a small bowl, combine all ingredients for topping and then cover to refrigerate.
2. Start the Instant Pot on the Sauté function and add oil when hot. Add garlic when the oil is hot and cook, stirring for 1-2 minutes until the garlic starts to brown. Add tomatoes and juices, hominy, salt, pepper, and frozen shrimp one after the other. Stir well to combine.
3. Select Cancel to stop sautéing. Then tightly close the lid with the steam release valve pointing to Sealing. Select Pressure Cook function and program the pot to cook for 1 minute. When the cook time is up, do a quick release of the pressure.

4. Add hot sauce as desired and ladle the soup into serving bowls. Serve with cumin cream and sprinkle with cilantro and side with the lime.

Yield: 6-8 servings.

Nutritional content per serving: Total fat: 6 g, Total Carbs: 7 g, Total Fiber: 3 g, Protein: 8 g, Calories: 104.

Sweet and Sour Shrimp

Creating sweet and sour sauce usually takes a great deal. However, the effort is handsomely rewarded with a tasty meal. Getting the timing right will require that you watch the number or weight of the shrimp.

Total cook time: 30 minutes.

Ingredients
- 1 cup canned pineapple chunks in juice (drained, plus ¼ cup juice from the can)
- ½ cup chicken broth (vegetable or fish broth can do)
- ¼ cup regular (or reduced-sodium) soy sauce or tamari
- ¼ cup granulated white sugar
- ¼ cup unseasoned rice vinegar (or 3 tbsp. apple cider vinegar)
- 1 tbsp. peeled and minced fresh ginger
- 2 tsp. peeled and minced garlic
- ¼ tsp. red pepper flakes
- 1 ½ lb. frozen shrimp (to be peeled and deveined, raw medium shrimp, 30-35 per pound)
- 1 lb. frozen unseasoned stir-fry vegetable (blend into 4 - 5 cups, any seasoning packet discarded)
- 2 tbsp. cornstarch

Instructions
1. Stir the pineapple chunks (without the juice) together with the next seven ingredients on the list up to and including red pepper flakes in an Instant Pot. Add the shrimp and vegetables and stir well. Then tightly close the lid with the steam release valve pointing to Sealing.
2. Select the Press Pressure Cook option and program to cook for 10 minutes. When the timer beeps, do a quick release of the pressure and carefully unlatch the lid when the valve drops to open the cooker.
3. Change the setting to Sauté and program to cook for 5 minutes. Bring the sauce to a simmer and whisk the reserved ¼ cup pineapple juice and cornstarch in a small bowl. Stir the mixture into the sauce and continue sautéing. Stir almost constantly for about 1 minute until thickened. Turn off the Sauté function. Use the mitts to remove the insert so that shrimp don't overcook in the pot. Pour the cooked shrimp in the pot with all sauce into a serving bowl.

Yield: 5 servings.

Nutritional content per serving: Total fat: 16 g, Total Carbs: 51 g, Dietary Fiber: 15 g, Protein: 12 g, Calories: 369.

CHAPTER 8: INSTANT POT DUO EVO PLUS CHICKEN/POULTRY RECIPES

Oh! My chicken and turkey!

I have practically nothing to say about these winged creature meats than to invite you to explore these recipes and others not listed in this chapter. They are just to show you that there's hardly an end to whatever you can do with chicken and turkey. The poultry meats are simply impossible to confine in a cage.

Enjoy your meal!

Fall Off the Bone Chicken

In just a little over 1 hour, this chicken will literally fall off the bone to your plate. You will find it to be the best bird meat you've made even if it's not the prettiest.

Total cook time: 70 minutes.

Ingredients

- 1 tbsp. packed brown sugar
- 1 tbsp. chili powder
- 1 tbsp. smoked paprika
- 1 tsp. freshly chopped thyme
- 1 whole small chicken (3 lb. to 4 lb.)
- Kosher salt
- Freshly ground black pepper (to taste)
- 1 tbsp. extra-virgin olive oil
- 2/3 cup low-sodium chicken broth
- 2 tbsp. freshly chopped parsley

Instructions

1. Whisk together the first four ingredients on the list in a small bowl. Then, pat the chicken dry using paper towels and season generously with pepper and salt. Rub the mixture all over the chicken.
2. Start the Instant Pot on Sauté mode and add oil once hot. Add the chicken, breast side down when the oil is heated. Sear for about 4 minutes until the skin is crispy. Using large tongs, flip the chicken and then pour the broth into the inner pot. Tightly secure lid with the steam release valve point to Sealing. Program to pressure cook for 25 minutes on high.
3. Once the cook time is up, wait for the natural pressure release. When the float valve drops, remove the lid and transfer the chicken without bones to a bowl where you will slice it after leaving it 10 minutes to firm up.
4. Serve warm, garnished with parsley.

Yield: Yield: 4 servings.

Nutritional content per serving: Calories: 302, Total Carbs: 13 g, Protein: 21 g, Total Fat: 19 g, Cholesterol: 88 mg, Dietary Fiber: 2g.

Chicken Shawarma

This Instant Pot version of Sharwama made with chicken is a quick and easy homemade healthy meal.

Total cook time: 30 minutes.

Ingredients
For Chicken Shawarma

- ¼ tsp. coriander powder
- ¼ tsp. cumin powder
- ½ tsp. paprika
- 1 tsp. cardamom powder
- ½ tsp. cinnamon powder or 3-inch piece of cinnamon stick
- ¼ tsp. cloves (to be powdered)
- ¼ tsp. nutmeg
- 1 ½ tsp. salt or to taste
- ¼ cup lemon juice
- ¼ cup yogurt
- 2 tbsp. garlic (to be minced)
- 2 lb. boneless skinless chicken thighs (to be cut into 2-inch strips)
- 2 bay leaves
- Chopped parsley for garnish
- Pita to serve

For Toppings: Lettuce, tomatoes (**Optional toppings:** cucumbers, feta cheese, French fries or sweet potato fries, hummus, sliced onions, pickled cucumbers.)

For Garlic Sauce / White Sauce

- ¼ cup plain Greek yogurt or whole milk yogurt
- 1 tbsp. mayonnaise
- 1/8 tsp. salt or to taste
- 1 tbsp. lemon juice
- ½ tsp. garlic (to be minced)
- ½ jalapeno pepper (to be finely chopped, optional)

Instructions
Chicken Shawarma

1. Combine the first 12 ingredients of Shawarma in a large mixing bowl and mix well to form a marinade. Add chicken and stir. Refrigerate for, at least, 2 hours or up to 8 hours or overnight.
2. Transfer the marinated chicken to the inner pot and add bay leaves. Stir well to combine. Tightly secure the lid with the steam release valve pointing to Sealing, pressure cook for 5 minutes. When the timer beeps, allow the natural release of pressure. You may in a hurried situation first do a 10-minute natural pressure release and do a quick release of the remaining pressure.
3. Transfer the chicken to a serving dish, using a slotted spoon. Drain well and sauce. (You may also brown the chicken by sautéing for a couple of minutes.)

Garlic Sauce / White Sauce

4. Combine all garlic sauce ingredients or white sauce in a bowl and whisk together until smooth. Set aside.
5. To assemble the chicken shawarma, slightly heat the pita for pliability. Then spread the sauce on the pita. Add lettuce and tomatoes. Add your favorite toppings. Then add chicken and garnish with chopped parsley.

Yield: 6 servings.

Nutritional content per serving: Calories: 279, Total Carbs: 18 g, Protein: 24 g, Total Fat: 13 g, Cholesterol: 53 mg, Dietary Fiber: 3 g

Southern BBQ Chicken

This poultry meal can make the main course for your dinner. It's interesting to many folks how barbecue turns out to be made in the Instant Pot. This Southern BBQ chicken will make a finger-licking-good dessert of the main course. Don't forget hot-cooked frozen broccoli, cauliflower, and carrot blend or even hot mashed potatoes while serving.

Total cook time: 40 minutes.

Ingredients
- 1 tbsp. oil
- 1 ½ lb. boneless skinless chicken thighs (to be cut into 1 ½-inch piece)
- ½ cup water
- 1 jar (15 oz.) Instant Pot Southern Barbeque Sauce

Instructions
1. Start the pot on the Sauté setting and heat oil when the message "Hot" displays. Add chicken and cook for 5 minutes while stirring frequently. Add water and barbeque sauce without stirring. Close the lid securely with the steam release valve turned to the "Sealing" position.
2. Select Pressure Cook function and program to cook for 6 minutes and program to cook on high. When the timer counts down to zero, carefully turn the steam release valve to Venting for a quick release of pressure. Once the pressure is all gone and the valve has dropped, carefully open the lid. Then serve warm.

Yield: 6 servings.

Nutritional content per serving: Calories: 300, Total Carbs: 16 g, Protein: 35 g, Total Fat: 14 g, Cholesterol: 180 mg, Dietary Fiber: 3 g.

Greens Lemon-Herb Chicken

Now that making the herb sauce is out of the way, you can readily green your chicken with a few simple ingredients and get a decently okay meal. Within some 30 minutes, your meal is done. The ensuing chicken could be served on pasta, beans, rice, or any grain. Your effort will be rewarded.

Total cook time: 31 minutes.

Ingredients

- 1 tbsp. oil
- 1 ½ lb. boneless, skinless chicken breasts (to be cut into strips)

- ½ cup water
- 1 jar (15 oz.) Instant Pot Zesty Lemon Herb Sauce

Instructions
1. Start the pot on the Sauté setting and heat oil when the message "Hot" displays. Add chicken and cook for 5 minutes while stirring frequently. Add water and the lemon herb sauce without stirring. Close the lid securely with the steam release valve turned to the Sealing position.
2. Select Pressure Cook function and set to cook for 6 minutes; program to high-pressure cooking. When the timer counts down to zero, carefully turn the valve to the Venting position for a quick release of pressure. Once the pressure is all gone and the valve has dropped, carefully opening lid and serve warm.

Yield: 4 servings.

Nutritional content per serving: Calories: 320, Total Carbs: 10 g, Protein: 33 g, Total Fat: 13 g, Cholesterol: 125 mg, Dietary Fiber: 7 g.

Thanksgiving-Inspired Pulled Turkey

Turkey tenderloins always work best since they shred into a pulled consistency. Yet, we can prove that a chunk of boneless skinless turkey breast can still be fine even though it might not be so easy to shred. You may cut it into three even pieces for the approximate size and shape of the tenderloins.

Total cook time: 45 minutes.

Ingredients
- ¾ cup chicken broth
- ½ cup whole berry cranberry sauce
- 2 tbsp. packed fresh sage leaves (to be finely chopped)
- 2 tsp. fresh thyme leaves
- 1 tsp. table salt (or to taste)
- 1 small sweet potato (to be peeled and shredded through large holes in a box grater)
- 2 ½ lb. boneless skinless turkey tenderloins

Instructions
1. Mix the first five ingredients on the list in the inner pot. Stir in the sweet potato shreds and then position the turkey in the sauce. Turn it to coat. Close the lid securely with the steam release valve turned to the Sealing position.
2. Select the Meat/Stew or Pressure Cook function and program to cook for 25 minutes on high pressure. When the timer counts down to zero, wait about 20 minutes for the natural release of pressure. Once the pressure is all gone and the valve has dropped, carefully unlatch the lid to open the pot.
3. Using two forks shred the meats in the pot and stir well to be coated with sauce. Then, set the lid askew over the Instant Pot for 6-9 minutes for the flavors to blend and the sauce to be absorbed by the turkey.

.Yield: 4 servings.

Nutritional content per serving: Calories: 186, Protein: 39 g, Total Fat: 2 g, Cholesterol: 83 mg, Dietary Fiber: 3 g.

Turkey Taco Lettuce Boats

Your views about tacos will change forever after trying out this turkey taco recipe. Use a large romaine lettuce leaf in place of taco shells. This home for your taco fixings is not only a healthy but also a cool way to enjoy tacos. With the crisp leaf, you've got a nice contrast.

Total cook time: 20 minutes.

Ingredients
- 1 tbsp. avocado oil
- 1 medium onion (to be peeled and diced)
- 2 large carrots (to be peeled and diced)
- 2 medium stalks celery (ends to be removed and diced)
- 2 cloves garlic (to be minced)
- 1 lb. lean ground turkey
- 1 tsp. chili powder
- 1 tsp. paprika
- 1 tsp. cumin
- ¼ tsp. black pepper (or to taste)
- ½ tsp. salt (or to taste)
- 1 cup chipotle salsa
- 12 large romaine leaves
- 1 medium avocado (to be peeled, pitted, and sliced)

Instructions
1. Start the pot on the Sauté setting and heat oil when the message "Hot" displays. After 1 minute add the diced onion, carrots, and celery plus garlic. Cook about 5 minutes, or until softened. Add the ground turkey and cook about 3 minutes, or until browned. Add the chili, paprika, cumin, pepper, salt, and salsa. Stir to combine and then cancel sautéing.
2. Firmly secure the lid with steam release valve pointing to Sealing. Select the Pressure Cook or Poultry function and program to cook for 15 minutes. When the timer counts down to zero, do a quick release pressure. When the float valve drops, unlock the lid and open.
3. Serve by spooning a portion of the taco meat into a romaine leaf. Top with avocado.

Yield: 4 servings.
Nutritional content per serving: Total fat: 18 g, Total Carbs: 18 g, Dietary Fiber: 8 g, Protein: 27 g, Calories: 339.

Chipotle Turkey and Sweet Potato Chili

Potatoes will always find their way around just about anything, including turkey. The chipotle with its dryness in the sauce will be absorbed by the sweetness of this potato to enhance the natural sumptuous flavor turkey. Check out the use of green peppers and red peppers here.

Total cook time: 20 minutes.

Ingredients
- 1 tbsp. olive oil
- 1 lb. 93%-fat-free ground turkey
- ½ cup chopped onions
- 3 garlic cloves (to be minced)
- ¾ lb. sweet potatoes (to be peeled, cut into ½-inch pieces)
- 1 jar (15 oz.) Instant Pot Smoky Chipotle Sauce
- 1 can (14 ½ oz.) diced tomatoes (undrained)
- 1 cup chopped green peppers
- 1 cup chopped red peppers
- ½ cup water
- 3 tbsp. tomato paste

Instructions
1. Start the pot on the Sauté setting for 7 min. When hot add oil and heat for 2 minutes. Add turkey and cook for 3 minutes, stirring frequently. Then add onions and garlic and cook while stirring for 2 minutes. Add the remaining ingredients and stir.
2. Securely close the lid and ensure that the pressure release valve turns to the Sealing position. Cook 10 minutes using Pressure Cook / Poultry setting. When the timer counts down to zero, use the Quick Pressure Release method to release steam. When the pin drops, unlatch and remove the lid. Then stir well and serve.

Yield: 8 servings.

Buffalo Style Turkey Meatballs

Anything buffalo is always a crowd-pleaser, especially when it has passed through the Instant Pot. The flavorful turkey meatballs in this recipe are healthy as they are low in calories. It's the appetizer or snacks that you'll love. It's also not going to be a bad anchor for a light meal.

Total cook time: 40 minutes.

Ingredients
For Meatball Mixture:
- 1 lb. ground turkey
- 1/3 cup panko breadcrumbs
- 1 egg
- 1 tsp. onion powder
- 1 tsp. kosher salt
- ½ tsp. pepper (or to taste)
- 1 tbsp. Buffalo-style hot sauce

Other Ingredients:
- 1 tbsp. olive oil
- ¼ cup chicken broth
- ½ cup Buffalo-style hot sauce

For serving: Ranch or blue cheese dressing or blue cheese crumbles, thinly sliced green

Instructions

1. Combine all of the meatball mixture ingredients in a medium bowl. Use wet hands to prevent sticking while shaping it into 18 meatballs.
2. Start the pot on the Sauté setting and heat olive oil when the message "Hot" appears. Add meatballs to the hot oil to brown on 3 sides, about 3 minutes per side. The meat will not be cooked through this time. You may work in batches to avoid crowding the pot. Transfer each browned meatballs to a shallow dish. Cover loosely with foil.
3. Deglaze the pot by adding broth and scraping brown bits from the bottom using a wooden spoon. Then stir in the half cup of hot sauce. Return the meatballs to the pot. Turn it once to coat. Select Cancel to turn the pot off.
4. Secure the lid tightly and ensure that the release valve is on the Sealing position. Then select Pressure Cook function and program to cook for 5 minutes. When the timer beeps, carefully do a quick release of the pressure. When the pin drops, open and serve hot. Garnish with your favorite dressing.

Yield: 5 servings.
Nutritional content per serving: Total fat: 8.2 g, Total Carbs: 32.7 g, Dietary Fiber: 3.2 g, Protein: 39.7 g, Cholesterol 91 mg, Calories: 365.

Turkey and Stuffing

Turkey with its stuffing will bring another unique taste. And parties in the combination would have had their tastes enhanced after going through a few moments in the Instant Pot. Chicken soup, stuffing mix, and green beans all combine to make this recipe happen.

Total cook time: 1 hour 20 minutes.

Ingredients
- 2 lb. uncooked turkey breast (to be cut into 4 pieces of 1-inch thick)
- 1 tsp. salt
- 1 tsp. pepper
- ¾ cup chicken broth
- 6 oz. stuffing mix (1 box)
- 10.5 oz. cream of chicken soup (1 can)
- 8 oz. sour cream plain Greek yogurt (or mayonnaise)
- 2 cups frozen green beans

Instructions
1. Season the turkey pieces with salt and pepper and layer evenly in the Instant Pot. Add broth to the pot. Lock the lid in place, ensuring that the release valve is closed, turning to the venting position. Select the Pressure Cook / Poultry function and program the Instant Pot to cook for 7 minutes on high pressure.
2. In the meantime, gently fold in stuffing mix, cream of soup, and sour cream together just until combined. Mix only slightly.
3. When the timer beeps, do a quick release of the pressure. Check if the turkey is fully cooked. If not, add 2 tablespoons of water and repeat the process of sealing the pot and pressure cook on high for an additional 2 minutes and do a quick release after 2 minutes.
4. Set frozen green beans evenly on the turkey without stirring it. Repeat the process of sealing the pot one more time and pressure cook again for 2 minutes.

Thereafter, do a quick release of the pressure. Repeat the same process of layering on the green beans. This time the pressure cooking time will be 4 minutes after sealing. But the pressure release method will still be quick.

5. Unlatch to open the lid and serve hot immediately with cranberry sauce as a side.

Yield: 6-8 servings.

Nutritional content per serving: Total fat: 6 g, Total Carbs: 7 g, Dietary Fiber: 3 g, Protein: 8 g, Calories: 104.

Ma Shu Turkey

Ma Shu Turkey is the best recipe to conclude this section of the poultry meat. With an unusual combination of ginger, cinnamon, and flour tortilla, the boneless turkey breast gets an uncommon beautiful taste. Even before it gets to your mouth the moment it's served, you'll start to savor the pleasantness of Ma Shu.

Total cook time: 15 minutes.

Ingredients
- 7 oz. plum sauce (1 jar, to be divided)
- ¼ cup orange juice (extracted from 1 medium orange)
- ¼ cup finely chopped onion
- 1 tbsp. minced fresh ginger
- ¼ tsp. salt (or to taste)
- ¼ tsp. ground cinnamon
- 1 lb. boneless turkey breast (to be cut into thin strips)
- 6 flour tortillas (7-inch)
- 3 cups coleslaw mix

Instructions
1. Combine the first 6 ingredients on the list in Instant Pot and mix very well. Add turkey breast and stir to coat.
2. Tightly secure the lid and have the steam release valve turned to the Sealing position. Select Pressure Cook / Poultry and program to cook for 4 minutes at high pressure. When the timer counts down to zero, carefully turn the pressure release valve to the Venting position for a quick release of pressure.
3. Start the Sauté function and cook 2 to 3 minutes, or until sauce thickens slightly and reduces. Spread the remaining sauce over tortillas and top with turkey and coleslaw mix. Then, fold the bottom edge of tortillas over as a filling. Also, fold in sides; roll up to completely enclose filling. Serve using the remaining cooking sauce as dipping.

Yield: 6 servings.

Nutritional content per serving: Total fat: 16 g, Total Carbs: 51 g, Dietary Fiber: 15 g, Protein: 12 g, Calories: 369.

CHAPTER 9: INSTANT POT DUO EVO PLUS GLUTEN-FREE, VEGETARIAN & KETO DIETS

Are you having a dietary restriction? Don't be quick to give up on the Instant Pot, concluding that it is not for you. Oh! Yeah! The Instant Pot Duo Evo Plus is for you too. It is suitable to cook most of the food that people with special diet requirements eat.

This is great news for those on gluten-free, vegetarian, and ketogenic diets. Your high-fat and energy-boosting recipes have their places in the Instant Pot.

The recipes sited in this chapter have been carefully selected and prepared by skillful chefs who have attested to the richness and nutritional values of restricted meals. They have reeled out a lot of health benefits derivable from cooking your food in the Instant Pot.

Try to see how you can work these into your menu even if you have to make a few adjustments for dietary reasons.

Black-Eyed Peas Summer Salad

This is a perfect dish for vegan, omnivore friends, and those on gluten-free diets. It can be a side dish a reserved as a prepping for later meals. You will find this salad very delicious. It's healthy and flavorful such that no one will notice that it's a special diet.

Total cook time: 30 minutes.

Ingredients
- 2 cups dried black-eyed peas (to be rinsed)
- 4 cups chicken broth
- 1 tsp. salt (or to taste)
- ¼ tsp. ground black pepper (or to taste)
- 1 medium cucumber (to be peeled, seeded, and diced)
- 2 Roma tomatoes (to be seeded and diced)
- ½ medium red onion (to be peeled and diced)
- 1 corn kernels
- ¼ cup crumbled feta cheese
- 2 tbsp. chopped fresh dill
- 2 tsp. olive oil

Instructions
1. Pour the peas and broth to the inner pot. Securely lock the lid and ensure that the steam release valve is pointing to the Sealing position. Press the Beans button with the default cook time of 30 minutes. When the timer counts down to zero, wait for 10 minutes of natural pressure release. Then, do a quick-release of the remaining pressure. When the float valve drops, unlock the lid and open. Drain the extra liquid, if any.

2. Transfer the peas to a bowl and allow it to cool for 10 minutes. Then add the remaining ingredients and toss to mix. Cover and keep in the fridge when cool for 30 minutes or overnight. Serve chilled.

Yield: 8 servings.

Chi-Town Italian Beef and Peppers

This is an exclusively gluten-free recipe that you can enjoy without traveling to Chicago. The thin slices of beef and slivered peppers together with giardiniera (chopped pickled veggies), takes the prominence in this meal. The sandwiches are wet as they have been dipped in gravy. Take note of all of that in the instructions below.

Total cook time: 65 minutes.

Ingredients
- ¼ cup olive oil
- 1 tbsp. Italian seasoning
- 1 tsp. garlic powder
- 1 tsp. smoked paprika
- ½ tsp. red pepper flakes
- 1 tsp. salt
- ½ tsp. ground black pepper
- 1 green bell pepper (to be seeded and sliced)
- 1 red bell pepper (to be seeded and sliced)
- 1 yellow bell pepper (to be seeded and sliced)
- 1 large yellow onion (to be peeled and sliced)
- 3 lb. boneless chuck roast (to be quartered)
- 4 cups beef broth
- 1 cup chopped jarred giardiniera (to be drained)

Instructions
1. In a large bowl, combine the 11 first ingredients up to and including quartered roast and then toss. Cover the mixture and refrigerate for at least 30 minutes to make marinade, or up to overnight.
2. Start the Instant Pot on the Sauté function and add the meat when hot. Add veggies and marinade. Sear each side of the meat for 5 minutes or until brown. Pour in the beef broth. Securely lock the lid and ensure that the steam release valve is pointing to the Sealing position.
3. Press the Pressure Cook / Beef button and program to cook for 60 minutes. When the timer counts down to zero, wait for 5 minutes of natural pressure release and then, do a quick release of the remaining pressure. When the float valve drops, unlock the lid and open. Strain the liquid and retain just about ¼ cup in the pot. Keep the strained liquid.
4. Transfer the meat to a cutting board and leave for 5 minutes. When the meat is cool and has firmed up, thinly slice and add back to the pot. Add the veggies and return the reserved liquid for moistening. Use a slotted spoon to transfer the meat and veggies to eight bowls and serve. You may serve in gluten-free buns or lettuce wraps. Wherever it is served, garnish with giardiniera.

Yield: 8 servings.

Porcupine Meatballs in Tomato Sauce

Can meatballs really be gluten-free? This is what you get when you cook the gluten-free meatballs and rice together in tomato sauce. You will be short of words when you find these porcupine meatballs in the Instant Pot. You will have mixed feelings about it being delicious and fun to cook.

Total cook time: 50 minutes.

Ingredients

For the Meatballs
- 1 lb. ground beef
- 1 large egg (to be slightly beaten)
- ½ cup finely chopped yellow onion
- 1/3 cup Arborio rice
- ¼ cup chopped fresh parsley
- Salt and black pepper (to taste)

For the Sauce
- 14.5 oz. diced tomatoes (1 can, undrained)
- 1 cup water
- 1 tsp. dried oregano
- ½ tsp. ground cinnamon
- ½ tsp. smoked paprika
- ¼ tsp. ground cloves
- Salt and black pepper (to taste)
- Chopped fresh parsley (for garnish, optional)

Instructions
1. Prepare the meatballs by combining all the meatballs ingredients in a large bowl. Mix until well combined and shape into 8 to 10 meatballs. Set in the Instant Pot in a single layer.
2. Next, prepare the sauce by combining all sauce ingredients in a medium bowl. Stir well to combine and pour over the meatballs.
3. Securely lock the lid and ensure that the steam release valve is pointing to the Sealing position. Select the Pressure Cook option and program to cook for 15 minutes at high pressure. When the timer counts down to zero, wait for the natural release of pressure. Once the float valve drops, unlock the lid and carefully open.
4. Transfer the meatballs to a serving bowl. Using an immersion blender, puree the sauce in the pot until the desired smoothness. Also, pour the puree over the meatballs.
5. Serve garnished with parsley.

Yield: 6 servings.

Vegetarian Chili

This is a pure vegetarian way of enjoying chili. Whichever way you made it, you will certainly derive what you want in a vegan meal in it. Dominated by beans and kernel corn, all other ingredients are a testimony to use in preaching the evangelism of vegetarianism. It's simply delicious.

Total cook time: 25 minutes.

Ingredients
- 1 tbsp. oil
- 1 medium red bell pepper (to be seeded and chopped)
- 1 medium yellow onion (to be chopped)
- 1 large sweet potato (to be cut into ½-inch chunks, about 2 cups)
- 1 cup water
- 1 can black beans (to be drained and rinsed, 15 ½ oz.)
- 1 can diced tomatoes (undrained, 14 ½ oz.)
- 1 cup frozen whole kernel corn
- 1 package chili seasoning mix (McCormick Original Chili Seasoning Mix recommended)

Instructions
1. Start the Instant Pot on the Sauté function and add oil when hot. When the oil is heated, add pepper and onion and cook for 3 minutes, stirring. Add sweet potatoes and cook for 2 minutes, stirring. Add water and then beans, stirring. Add corn, tomatoes, and seasoning mix.
2. Securely lock the lid and ensure that the steam release valve is pointing to the Sealing position. Select the Pressure Cook option and program to cook for 7 minutes. When the timer counts down to zero, do a quick release of the pressure. Open the lid once the pressure inside the pot is completely released.
3. Serve immediately and enjoy!

Yield: 6 servings.

Lemon Ginger Broccoli and Carrots

Here is another Vegan diet of fresh ginger that gives a zesty bite to broccoli and carrots, two familiar vegetables. Ginger is a flavor enhancer for a lot of dishes apart from its strong anti-inflammatory properties. Combining this with garlic gives you all you need to enjoy your broccoli and carrots.

Total cook time: 25 minutes.

Ingredients
- 1 tbsp. avocado oil
- 1-inch fresh ginger (to be peeled and thinly sliced)
- 1 clove of garlic (to be minced)
- 2 broccoli crowns (stems to be removed and cut into large florets)
- 2 large carrots (to be peeled and thinly sliced)
- ½ tsp. kosher salt
- ½ large lemon (to be juiced)
- ¼ cup water

Instructions

1. Start the Instant Pot on the Sauté function and add oil when hot and heat 2 minutes. Add the ginger and garlic and continue sautéing 1 minute more. Add broccoli, carrots, and salt, stirring each time. Press the Cancel button to stop sautéing. Add the lemon and water and deglaze by using a wooden spoon to scrape any brown bits.
2. Securely lock the lid and ensure that the steam release valve is pointing to the Sealing position. Select the Pressure Cook option and program to cook for 2 minutes. When the timer counts down to zero, do a quick release of the pressure. Once the float valve drops, unlatch to open the lid.
3. Serve immediately.

Yield: 6 servings.

Nutritional content per serving: Total fat: 2g, Total Carbs: 10g, Dietary Fiber: 3g, Protein: 3 g, Calories: 67.

Coconut Curry Lentil Chickpea Bowls With Kale

The life vegan is one to be cherished or even coveted. If there is anything like healthy comfort food, this vegan dish is what fits whatever description it would have. You will definitely feel happy as you savor warm spices and lick the creamy texture. This recipe is super easy to prepare. So it can be a part of your regular rotation.

Total cook time: 20 minutes.

Ingredients
- ¾ cup red lentils
- 15 oz. diced tomatoes (with garlic and onion with juices, 1 can)
- 13.66 oz. unsweetened lite coconut milk (1 can)
- 1 cup vegetable broth
- 1 tbsp. curry powder
- 1 tsp. peeled and grated fresh ginger
- 1 tsp. turmeric
- 1 tsp. salt (or to taste)
- 15 oz. can chickpeas (to be drained and rinsed, 1 can)
- 4 cups deveined kale (to be finely chopped)
- 1 tbsp. lime juice
- 1/3 cup roughly chopped fresh cilantro leaves and stems

Instructions
1. Combine all the ingredients in the Instant Pot, except the kale, lime, and cilantro leaves. Stir well to combine.
2. Securely lock the lid and ensure that the steam release valve is pointing to the Sealing position. Select the Pressure Cook option and program to cook for 8 minutes. When the timer counts down to zero, wait for the natural release of pressure. Once the float valve drops, unlatch to open the lid.
3. Add kale and lime juice and stir well. Ladle into bowls and serve with cilantro as a topping.

Yield: 4 servings.

Nutritional content per serving: Total fat: 8g, Total Carbs: 48g, Dietary Fiber: 12g, Protein: 15 g, Calories: 328.

Buffalo Cauliflower Bites

These spicy buffalo-flavored cauliflower bites will cause you to bid farewell to the wings for now if you ever tried them. They are rich in flavor. More important is the additional health benefits offered by the cauliflowers even when not buffalo-flavored. What is more, it's a vegan meal.

Total cook time: 10 minutes.

Ingredients
- 1 head cauliflower (large, to be cut into large pieces)
- ½ cup buffalo hot sauce
- 1 cup water

Instructions
1. Place a steam rack inside the Instant Pot with water. Place the cauliflower in a medium bowl. Add the buffalo hot sauce and toss to evenly coat. Lower the bowl on the steam rack. Secure the lid.
2. Securely lock the lid and ensure that the steam release valve is pointing to the Sealing position. Select the Pressure Cook option and program to cook for 2 minutes. When the timer counts down to zero, carefully do a quick-release pressure. Once the float valve drops, unlatch to open the lid.
3. Serve with toothpicks in 5 plates.

Yield: 5 servings.

Nutritional content per serving: Total Carbs: 10g, Dietary Fiber: 4g, Protein: 4 g, Calories: 52.

Mac and Cheese

Macaroni and cheese are common as a vegan meal. But the recipe here is a keto diet variation. So it's ideal during those moments of craving for those on keto. This recipe replaces macaroni with cauliflower. Thus, while capturing the desired flavor and texture together with comfort food classic, you'll not be knocked out of ketosis.

.Total cook time: 10 minutes.

Ingredients
- 4 tbsp. grass-fed butter (to be softened)
- 1 cup full-fat Cheddar cheese (to be shredded)
- 1 cup full-fat Monterey Jack cheese (to be shredded)
- 1 head cauliflower (to be chopped)
- ½ cup heavy whipping cream
- ½ cup full-fat Parmesan cheese (to be grated)
- ½ tsp. cayenne pepper (to be ground)
- ½ tsp. freshly ground black pepper
- ½ tsp. kosher salt
- 2 cups filtered water

Instructions
1. Pour the water into the Instant Pot with the trivet inserted. Combine all the 9 ingredients in a large bowl and mix thoroughly. Transfer the mixture into a greased

Instant Pot-compatible dish. Lower the dish onto the trivet and cover loosely with foil.

2. Tightly secure the lid and ensure that the steam release valve is pointing to the Sealing position. Select the Pressure Cook option and program to cook for 5 minutes on high pressure. When the timer counts down to zero, carefully turn the steam release to Venting for a quick-release pressure. Once the float valve drops, unlatch to open the lid.

3. Remove the dish and serve when cool. Enjoy!

Yield: 4 servings.

Nutritional content per serving: Total fat: 41.6g, Total Carbs: 5.8g, Dietary Fiber: 1.8g, Protein: 24 g, Calories: 489.

Creme Brulee

The keto-ers will love this Brulee. It's universal no longer a French dessert. It serves well as a perfect way to end a romantic dinner. Don't be scared of what you know about the traditional crème brûlée. This recipe has carefully excluded the dreaded sugar to make it keto-adapted. Dark berries are there to give some more antioxidants.

Total cook time: 15 minutes.

Ingredients
- 2 egg yolks
- 1 cup. heavy whipping cream
- 1 tsp. vanilla extract
- ½ cup Swerve confectioners (or more, to taste)
- 1/8 tsp. salt
- 1 cup filtered water

Instructions
1. Pour water into the inner pot and insert the trivet. Combine egg yolks, cream, vanilla extract, Swerve, and salt in a large bowl and mix thoroughly. Evenly pour the mixture into 5 greased Instant Pot-compatible ramekins. Lower the ramekins on the trivet and cover loosely with foil.

2. Tightly secure the lid and ensure that the steam release valve is pointing to the Sealing position. Select the Pressure Cook option and program to cook for 6 minutes on high pressure. When the timer counts down to zero, allow 10 minutes of natural pressure release and then carefully turn the steam release to Venting for a quick release the remaining pressure. Once the float valve drops, unlatch to open the lid.

3. Take the ramekins out of the pot and allow them cool. Then, serve and enjoy!

Yield: 5 servings.

Nutritional content per serving: Total fat: 10g, Total Carbs: 0.9g, Protein: 2.7 g, Calories: 110.

Crab Bisque

Crab bisque is what serves as a more delicious and nutritious dinner when you are already in ketosis. It's a very nice meal for the keto diet when paired with fresh asparagus.

Steamed broccoli will produce the same effect with it. If you garnish the bisque with some tarragon or paprika, you will get a grand taste.

Total cook time: 10 minutes.

Ingredients

- 4 tbsp. grass-fed butter (to be softened)
- 3 cups grass-fed bone broth
- 8 oz. full-fat cream cheese (to be softened)
- 2 stalks celery (to be chopped)
- 1 lb. frozen crab meat (to be thawed)
- 1 tsp. Old Bay seasoning
- ½ tsp. cayenne pepper (to be ground)
- ½ tsp. freshly ground black pepper (or to taste)
- ½ tsp. kosher salt (or to taste)
- ¼ cup bell peppers (to be chopped)
- ¼ cup heavy whipping cream
- 4 oz. onion (to be thinly sliced ¼ small)
- 14 oz. sugar-free (or low-sugar, crushed tomatoes 1 cup)

Instruction

1. Start the Instant Pot on the Sauté mode and add butter when hot. Once the butter melts, add the bone broth. Also, add the cream cheese and mix. Add the rest of the ingredients in the listed order, stirring each time.
2. Tightly secure the lid and ensure that the steam release valve is pointing to the Sealing position. Select the Pressure Cook option and program to cook for 3 minutes on low pressure. When the timer counts down to zero, do a quick release by carefully turning the steam release to Venting. Once the float valve drops, unlatch to open the lid. If you want it smoother, use an immersion blender to puree the soup until desired consistency.
3. Remove the bisque and serve immediately. Enjoy!

Yield: 4 servings.

Nutritional content per serving: Total fat: 35.1g, Total Carbs: 10.7g, Protein: 13 g, Calories: 415.

CHAPTER 10: INSTANT POT DUO EVO PLUS SLOW COOKER RECIPES

One of the benefits of the Instant Pot is that it's an all in one cooker. Its function of slow cooking entices a lot of people to it. This is more pronounced with the Instant Pot Duo Evo Plus as you will see in the recipes packed into this chapter. Remember that slow cooking is one of its 9 smart programs.

But what slow cooker meal can you really cook in the Instant Pot Duo Evo Plus? Simply put; it's just about anything you can cook on a slow cooker. So you have examples such as beefs, cookies, pancakes, and lasagna, among others here that you can try and even vary the versions.

Just put your recipes together and go to work or bed. Come back later and enjoy your slow-cooked delicacies.

Note that in slow cooking, the steam release valve should generally be left on the Venting position. It's not much of a pressure cooking.

Slow-Cooked Whiskey-Molasses Shredded Beef

Beef is the right way to start the discussion of slow cooking. We have shredded it here. Molasses is there to give the usually honey taste. But we're not getting it just from the burnt sugar. It's whiskey molasses. Even the tender tomatoes can withstand long cooking as you'll see here.

Total cook time: 90 minutes.

Ingredients

- 2 ½ -3 lb. beef bottom round roast (or beef chuck center roast, to be cut into 1-inch pieces)
- ½ cup beef broth
- ½ cup whiskey
- ¼ cup + 2 tbsp. cider vinegar (to be divided)
- 6 oz. tomato paste (1 can)
- 4 tbsp. brown sugar (to be packed, divided)
- ¼ cup molasses
- 1 ½ tsp. salt (or to taste)
- ½ tsp. red pepper (to be ground)
- 1 tbsp. Dijon mustard
- 2 cups carrots (to be shredded)
- 2 cups Granny Smith apples (to be diced)

Instructions

1. Add beef roast and beef broth in the Instant Pot. Lock the lid in place with the steam release valve pointing to Sealing. Select the Slow Cook /Beef or Stew setting and program to cook for 90 minutes on high pressure. When the timer beeps, signifying the end of cook time, carefully do a quick-release by turning the steam release valve to Venting. Once the pin drops, carefully remove the lid.

2. Shred the beef and return to the Instant Pot. Add the cooking liquid, whiskey, ¼ cup of cider vinegar, tomato, 2 tablespoons of brown sugar, molasses, pepper, and salt in a small saucepan and mix thoroughly while simmering for about 20-25 minutes, or until desired consistency. Add the sauce to the pot and combine with the shredded beef.
3. Make the slaw by combining the remaining 2 tablespoons of cider vinegar, 2 tablespoons of brown sugar, and mustard in a medium bowl. Add carrots and apples. Mix well and season with salt and black pepper as desired. Store in the fridge for a few hours and serve the slaw with the beef.

Yield: 8 servings.

Slow Cooker Giant Chocolate Chip Cookie

You could mistake this giant cookie for the regular chocolate chip cookie due to its taste. You know what? It's sugar-free and low carb; great for ketoers again for the sweet treat! Warm and gooey, it's filled with crunchy walnuts.

Total cook time: 4 hours.

Ingredients
- Non-stick coconut oil spray
- 2/3 cup sweetener (erythritol and oligosaccharide blend granular recommended)
- 5½ tbsp. butter
- 1 large egg
- 1 tsp. blackstrap molasses
- ½ tsp. vanilla extract
- 1¼ cup almond flour
- 1 tbsp. coconut flour
- 1 ½ tsp. baking powder
- 1/8 tsp. fine grind sea salt
- ½ tsp. xanthan gum
- ½ cup sugar-free stevia-sweetened chocolate chips
- ¼ cup chopped walnuts

Instructions
1. Line the inner pot of the Instant Pot with parchment paper and spray with oil spray. Set aside. Combine sweetener and butter in a large bowl and cream until thoroughly combined, using a stand mixer or hand mixer. Add the egg, blackstrap molasses, and vanilla extract. Mix a little more until thoroughly combined. Set aside.
2. Combine the almond and coconut flours in a separate large bowl. Add baking powder, salt, and gum. Stir until blended.
3. Combine the dry ingredients and the wet ingredients and mix very well. Fold in the chocolate and walnuts.
4. Add the dough to the inner pot and spread by using a rubber spatula to press the dough into the bottom. Make sure it covers the bottom of the pot completely without any gaps.
5. Securely lock the lid but leave the steam release valve in the Venting position. Select the Slow Cook / Custom function and program to cook for 4 hours on high.

When the timer counts down to zero, unlatch to open the lid and use tongs or mitts to transfer the inner pot to a cooling rack. The cookie will still be soft and doughy. Wait for about 30 minutes for the cookie to cool in the inner pot. It should reach the room temperature by or before then.

6. Transfer the cookie to a plate; slice into 8 wedges, and serve warm. You can transfer to an airtight container and store in the fridge for up to 6 days.

Yield: 8 servings.

Nutritional content per serving: Total fat: 20g, Net Carbs: 5g, Protein: 5 g, Calories: 210.

Slow Cooker German Pancake

There is no much of German in this pancake. It's better described by the process it goes through. It's a slow cooker pancake. This is obvious in the ingredients that make it up. And as you will see, the instructions are as common as what you're familiar with.

Total cook time: 90 minutes.

Ingredients
- 4 large eggs
- ½ cup unsweetened almond milk
- ½ tsp. lemon juice
- 1 tsp. vanilla extract
- 1 cup almond flour
- ¼ cup sweetener (erythritol and oligosaccharide blend granular, recommended)
- ½ tsp. baking powder
- ¼ tsp. fine grind sea salt
- 3 tbsp. melted butter (to be divided)
- 2 tbsp. no-sugar-added berry jam

Instructions
1. Add the first 4 ingredients on the list in a large bowl and whisk well to combine. Set aside. Combine the next 4 ingredients on the list in a medium bowl and mix well. Combine the dry ingredients with the wet ingredients and mix thoroughly until no lumps remain in the batter.
2. Start the Instant Pot on the Sauté mode and add 1 tablespoon of butter to coat the bottom. Add the batter when the butter is warm. Cover and securely lock the lid but leave the steam release valve in the Venting position. Select Slow Cook function and program to cook for 90 minutes on High. When the timer beeps to signify the end of cook time, carefully open the lid. Check the doneness of the pancake by inserting a toothpick into the center. If it's done, the toothpick will come out clean.
3. Transfer the inner pot to a tray and wait a while for it to cool a bit. Use a spatula to carefully loosen the pancake edges from the sides of the pot. Transfer to a large plate and flip over so that the browned side of the pancake will face up.
4. Slice into 6 wedges and drizzle each wedge with 1 teaspoon of the melted butter. Also, top with 1 teaspoon each of the berry jam. Then serve warm.

Yield: 6 servings.

Nutritional content per serving: Total fat: 11g, Net Carbs: 3g, Protein: 5g, Calories: 138.

Slow Cooker Chicken Fajita

This dish of strips and spicy marinated chicken in a soft flour tortilla is often served with salad or a savory filling. But the sky is actually the limit of how fajita can be cooked and served. Chicken is the base of this fajita. And it will go through the slow-cooking process.

Total cook time: 370 minutes.

Ingredients
- 1 tbsp. olive oil
- 2 tsp. fajita seasoning
- ½ tsp. chicken base
- 2 cloves garlic minced
- 2 boneless, skinless chicken breasts (3 oz.)
- 14.5 oz. diced tomatoes (1 can)
- ½ onion (to be sliced)
- ½ yellow bell pepper (to be sliced)
- ½ red bell pepper (to be sliced)
- 1 whole-wheat tortilla
- ¼ avocado (to be sliced)
- ¼ cup cilantro
- 1 lime wedge

Instructions
1. Mix the olive oil with fajita seasoning, chicken base, and garlic and then rub the mixture into the breasts. Pour half of the diced tomatoes into the pot. Add the onions, chicken, and peppers. Then, top with the remaining tomatoes.
2. Securely close the lid but have the vent remain open. Select the Slow Cook / Poultry option and program to cook for 6 hours on low. When the timer counts down to zero, open carefully and shred the chicken breasts using two forks. Fill with avocado, cilantro, and the lime wedge. Then serve.

Yield: 2 servings.

Slow Cooker Peanut Butter Fudge

With a subtle hint of butter from peanut, this fudge is chocolaty. Again, here's another sugar-free recipe that your friends will think it's sugar-packed. It's so delicious. The effect will not be too conspicuous if you use your favorite nut butter in place of peanut butter.

Total cook time: 125 minutes.

Ingredients
- 1 cup low-carb chocolate chips
- 8 oz. cream cheese
- ¼ cup erythritol
- ¼ cup no-sugar-added peanut butter
- 1 tsp. vanilla extract

Instructions
1. Place the 5 ingredients in the inner pot.

2. Securely cover but leave the steam release valve on the Venting position. Select the Slow Cook /Custom option and program to cook for 60 minutes on low. When the cook time ends, mix the mixture to smooth. Cook for 30 minutes more on Slow Cook mode.
3. Transfer the mixture to 8-inch by 8-inch parchment-lined pan. When cool, refrigerate for 2 hours. Slice and serve.

Yield: 6 servings.

Kale Slow Cook Spinach and Goat Cheese Lasagna

Any time a mention is made of lasagna in a recipe, the next thing chefs look for is the meat. In this recipe, it's the cheese that steals the show; and goat cheese for that matter. Spinach and Kale are the ones playing the role of vegetables in this Slow Cook recipe.

Total cook time: 2 hours.
Ingredients
- 1 tsp. extra-virgin olive oil
- 1 ¾ cups chopped onion
- 1 cup diced Zucchini
- ½ cup grated carrot
- 2 cloves garlic (to be chopped)
- ½ tsp. salt (or to taste)
- ½ tsp. freshly ground black pepper
- 28 oz. crushed tomatoes (undrained, 1 can)
- Cooking spray
- 1 cup chopped basil
- ¾ cup part-skim ricotta cheese
- 20 oz. chopped spinach (frozen, thawed, drained, and squeezed dry)
- 2 oz. goats cheese (roughly ¼ cup)
- 8 gluten-free lasagna noodles
- 1 oz. Parmesan cheese (to be shredded fresh, about ¼-cup)
- Basil leaves (optional)

Instructions
1. Heat a saucepan over medium heat and add oil when hot. Swirl to coat. Add onion, zucchini, and carrot. Cook for 5 minutes, stirring constantly. Add garlic; cook 1 minute, stirring constantly. Add salt, pepper, and tomatoes and stir. Bring to a simmer and cook for 5 minutes while stirring occasionally.
2. Coat the Instant Pot with cooking spray. In a medium bowl, mix together basil, ricotta, spinach, and goat cheese and add to the pot. Add ½ cup of spinach mixture into the cooker and spread. Set carefully 1/3 of lasagna noodles over the mixture, breaking noodles to size to fit in the pot. Add the remaining 10 ounces of spinach mixture and 1 cup of tomato mixture. (Don't cover the noodles completely.)
3. Cover and lock the lid in place and ensure that the steam release handle is turned to the Venting position. Select the Slow Cook / Custom function program to cook for 2 hours on low.
4. When the timer counts down to zero, carefully unlatch and open. Then sprinkle with Parmesan cheese and cover. Wait 15 minutes for it to cool a bit before serving. Serve garnished with basil leaves, if using.

Yield: 6 servings.

Slow Cook Maple French Toast Casserole

Slow cooking the sandwiched bread gives you all the time to attend to other pressing needs before mealtime. It also allows maple, cinnamon, and nutmeg to give out all in them to the casserole for those who want to eat immediately after cooking.

Total cook time: 90 minutes.

Ingredients
- Cooking spray
- 12 slices sandwich bread (to be cut into 1-inch pieces)
- 4 eggs (to be lightly beaten)
- ½ cup maple syrup
- 1 tsp. cinnamon
- ½ tsp. salt
- ¼ tsp. grated nutmeg
- 1/8 tsp. ground cloves
- 2 cups milk (reduced fat 2%)
- 1 tsp. powdered sugar

Instructions
1. Coat the inner pot with cooking spray and place the bread inside. Add the next 6 ingredients up to and including nutmeg in a medium bowl. Add milk and whisk well until well blended. Next, add the mixture to the bread in the pot and press gently with a spoon so that all bread pieces are coated.
2. Lay 10 ½-inch long aluminum foil piece on the top of the inner pot. Gradually smooth it down the pot side. Trim off the pointed side of the foil to make all sides even. Next, tightly tuck the foil under the rim.
3. Return the inner pot to the base and tightly close the lid with the steam release hand facing the Venting position. Select the Slow Cook / Custom function and program to cook for 90 minutes on low. When the cook time is up, carefully open to remove the bread.
4. Sprinkle with powdered sugar and serve warm. Enjoy!

Yield: 8 servings.

Slow Cook Steel-Cut Oatmeal With Apples

The beauty of the slow cooking function of the Instant Pot Duo Evo Plus is exhibited in this oatmeal with apples. You can make your breakfast while sleeping. Isn't that wonderful? Check it out!

Total cook time: 6 hours.

Ingredients
- 2 cups apple diced (such as Granny Smith, about 1 lb.)
- 1 cups steel-cut oats gluten-free (such as Bob's Red Mill)
- 3 ½ cups water
- ¼ cup honey (or liquid sweetener of choice such as maple syrup, or agave for vegan options, to taste)
- ¼ tsp. salt

- ½ tsp. allspice ground
- 7 oz. coconut milk (light ½ can)
- Cashews nuts (to be toasted, optional)
- Granny Smith apple (to be diced for topping, optional)

Instructions

1. Rub the inner pot of the Instant Pot with oil to coat and combine the apple with the next 6 ingredients. Lock the lid in place and have the steam release handle turned to the Venting position. Select the Slow Cook / Custom option and adjust the cook time to 6 hours on high. And go to bed.
2. Allow a natural pressure release to let out the pressure completely (that is if you woke up before that happens). Before serving, stir well and garnish with toasted cashews (if using) and additional diced apple (if desired). Enjoy!

Yield: 5 servings.

Nutritional content per serving: Total fat: 14g, Total Carbs: 17g, Fiber: 12 g, Protein: 16 g, Cholesterol 90 mg, Calories: 100.

Chipotle Braised Short Ribs

The short rib of beef can take longer to cook. So if you have plenty of matters to attend to, you can return to your Instant Pot Duo Evo Plus after 5 hours to conclude your cooking. It will take more out of your chipotle or jalapeno and increase the tenderness of your meat.

Total cook time: 5 hours.

Ingredients

- 3 lb. beef short ribs
- 1 tbsp. vegetable oil
- ½ tsp. black pepper
- ¼ tsp. salt
- 1 cup white onions (to be diced)
- 28 oz. crushed tomatoes (1 can)
- 5 medium poblano peppers (to be roasted, peeled, seeded, and cut into ¼-inch thick strips)
- 1-2 chipotle peppers in adobo sauce (to be finely chopped)
- White onion (to be chopped)
- Cilantro (to be chopped)
- Lime wedges (optional)

Instructions

1. Season the beef ribs with black pepper and salt in the Instant Pot. Add onion, crushed tomatoes, poblano peppers, and chopped chipotle peppers to the beef. Stir well to combine.
2. Lock the lid in place and have the steam release handle turned to the Venting position. Select the Slow Cook / Rib option and adjust the cook time to 5 hours on low. When time is up, use natural pressure release to let out the pressure completely. Remove beef, which should be fork tender by now and keep warm.
3. Skim fat off and spoon the cooking liquid over beef. Serve sprinkled with chopped onion and cilantro to taste. Then garnish with lime wedges.

Yield: 5 servings.

Slow Cook Marinated Flank Steak with Cranberry-Raspberry Salsa

Flank steak with cranberry/raspberry can taste uniquely when marinated. And 10 hours of slow cooking can do the marinating more than anything else.

Total cook time: 10 hours.

Ingredients
- 2 ½ tbsp. lime juice (fresh, about 2 limes)
- ¼ cup chili sauce
- 2 drops hot pepper sauce (such as Tabasco)
- 1 oz. taco seasoning 1 package (low sodium)
- 1 lb. flank steak (1 steak, to be trimmed)
- ½ cup sliced scallions (in 2-inch pieces)
- ¼ cup cilantro sprigs
- ½ tbsp. chopped and seeded Jalapeno pepper
- ½ tsp. ground cumin
- 6 oz. cranberry-raspberry crushed fruit (1 carton)
- Cilantro (fresh, optional)
- 8 tortillas (8-inch)

Instructions
1. Combine 1/8 cup of lime juice, chili sauce, pepper sauce, and taco seasoning in the inner pot. Add steak and turn to coat.
2. Lock the lid in place and have the steam release handle turned to the Venting position. Select the Slow Cook / Beef option and adjust the cook time to 1 hour on low. When the cook time is up, use the natural pressure release method to let out the pressure completely and stir gently. Then repeat the same process and this time program it to cook for 9 hours on less.
3. Meanwhile, set scallions, cilantro, and jalapeño in a food processor. Puree 5 times or until finely chopped. Then add the remaining ½ tablespoon of lime juice, ground cumin, and cranberry-raspberry. Process all until is smooth.
4. Ladle the mixture into a bowl and cover. Then refrigerate. When the timer counts down to zero, remove steak from the pot and discard the cooking liquid. Chop the steak into bite-sized pieces and garnish with cilantro. Warm the tortillas as directed in the package instruction.
5. Spread read 1 tablespoon over each tortilla and spoon ¼ cup of shredded steak down the center of each tortilla. Roll up.

Yield: 8 servings.

CHAPTER 11: INSTANT POT DUO EVO PLUS DESSERTS & CAKES

We all love desserts that we can nibble on after our lunch or dinner when we have the time to relax. If the Instant Pot Duo Evo Plus can make our breakfast, lunch, and dinner, it should be able to make our desserts. So we've got a number of them in this chapter to stimulate your imagination.

Cakes take a large percentage of what is known world over as desserts. So this chapter gives a few examples of cake recipes you will want to try your dexterous hands on. You can enjoy the presence of berries, chocolates, other ingredients that adds color to the cakes.

Maple Bread Pudding

Pudding is always a good dessert regardless of whatever it is made of. However, when it is in the company with maple bread, it takes another garb. The taste comes out better when you let it pass through the Instant Pot Duo Evo Plus.

Total cook time: 40 minutes.

Ingredients

- 4 slices bread (any kind, torn into 1-inch pieces)
- 2 eggs
- 1¼ cup milk
- ¼ cup brown sugar
- 1/3 cup maple syrup (or more brown sugar)
- 1/8 tsp. salt (or to taste)
- 1/8 tsp. nutmeg (optional)
- ½ tsp. vanilla
- ½ cup nuts raisins (optional, chocolate chips or your favorite)

Instructions

1. Combine all ingredients, except bread and whisk together. Pour the mixture over the bread and soak for a few minutes. Spray a cake pan with cooking spray. Then transfer the whole mixture into the pan. Cover it with tin foil.
2. Pour 1½ cups of water in the Instant Pot and lower the trivet. Place the pudding on the trivet. Tightly secure the lid, ensuring that the steam release valve is set to the Sealing position. Press the Pressure Cook and turn the knob to set the cook time to 25 minutes.
3. When the pot beeps to signify the end of cook time, wait for 10 minutes of natural pressure release. Then, carefully flip the valve from Sealing to Venting to quickly release the remaining pressure. When the pin drops, unlatch the lid to open the pot. Transfer the pudding to the countertop and remove its tin foil. Allow it cool for a few minutes before inverting onto a plate. Then serve warm or refrigerate to serve chilled with any of whipped cream, ice cream, or caramel sauce.

Yield: 4 servings.

Vanilla-Scented Rice Pudding

Rice pudding provides both comfort food and sophistication all in just one dish. With its subtly sweetened fragrant, the vanilla pudding comes out creamy and rich whether or not it is over the top. In a flash of less than 10 minutes, it's ready in your pot. It's a good one to quickly satisfy your cravings.

Total cook time: 8 minutes.

Ingredients
Dry ingredients
- ¼ tsp. sea salt (or to taste)
- ¼ tsp. cinnamon
- ¼ cup brown sugar
- 1 whole vanilla bean split along one side
- 3 cups Arborio (or short-grain white) rice
- ¾ cup raisins

For cooking and serving
- 4 ½ cups water
- ½ cup heavy cream (or coconut cream)

Instructions
1. Layer all the dry ingredients in a jar in the listed order, making sure that all is complete. Pour all of the jarred ingredients in the inner pot and add water. Stir well to mix.
2. Tightly secure the lid, ensuring that the steam release valve is set to the Sealing position. Press Pressure Cook / Custom and set the cook time to 8 minutes.
3. When the pot beeps to signify the end of cook time, wait for 10 minutes of natural pressure release. Then, carefully flip the valve from Sealing to Venting to quickly release the remaining pressure. When the pin drops, unlatch the lid to open the pot.
4. Wait for 10 minutes before serving.

Yield: 8 servings.

Brandy-Soaked Cheater Cherry Pie

You can resist the cherry pie if you are a fan of pies. Even if you don't like to bake, this brandy-soaked cherry pie is for you. It makes you one of the cheaters on the pie. The filling is quite easy. Just have the right combination of those delicious cherries with frozen fillo shells, you're good to go.

Total cook time: 15 minutes.

Ingredients

- 2 lb. cherries (to be pitted)
- 1/3 cup brandy
- 2/3 cup sugar
- 3 tbsp. cornstarch
- Pinch salt (to taste)

- ½ juice of lime
- oz. mini fillo shells (2 boxes 1.9 oz. each)

Instructions
1. Combine cherries and brandy in a large bowl and soak for 30 minutes; stir occasionally.
2. Start the Instant Pot on the Sauté mode on low. When the pot is hot, pour cherries together with the liquid. Add sugar and stir. Do the same to the cornstarch, salt, and lime juice. Continue sautéing for 10 to 12 minutes, or until thickened. Stir frequently to avoid burning anything.
3. Wait for a few minutes to allow it cool before spooning the filling into the fillo shells.

Yield: 6 servings.

Nutrition content per serving: Calories: 288; Total fat: 3g; Total Carbs: 61g; Dietary fiber: 3g; Protein: 4g.

Family Size Buttermilk Pancake

For a moderate family of, 5 the moderate size, this is the buttermilk pancake. Call it the usual pancake, you'll be fine. But peruse the recipe carefully and determine certain deviations from the norm. It is the variation that brought it a place here as a dessert recipe.

Total cook time: 50 minutes.

Ingredients
- 1½ cups flour
- 1 tsp. baking powder
- ¼ tsp. salt
- 1 cup buttermilk
- 2 tbsp. butter (to be melted)
- 1 cup water
- 2 large eggs
- 3 tbsp. sugar
- 2 tbsp. vegetable shortening or butter
- Favorite pancake toppings

Instructions
1. Combine flour, baking powder, and salt in a mixing bowl and whisk together. Add buttermilk, butter, water, eggs, and sugar in another bowl and whisk well. Stir the mixture into the dry ingredients and mix thoroughly until well combined. Add shortening or butter into the pot and spread on the bottom and sides up to 2 inches. Then pour in the batter.
2. Tightly secure the lid, ensuring that the steam release valve is set to the Sealing position. Select the Pressure Cook or Cake setting and program the cook time to 8 minutes (or use the default time of cake). When the pot beeps to signify the end of cook time, wait for 10-minute of natural pressure release. Then, carefully flip the valve from Sealing to Venting to quickly release the remaining pressure. When the pin drops, unlatch the lid to open the pot.
3. Run a rubber spatula around the pancake edge to remove pancake and invert onto a serving plate. Cut into 5 wedges and serve with favorite toppings.

Yield: 5 servings.

Pumpkin Pie Custard

This again is for pie fans. Pumpkin pie is what you can snack on after your meal. However, many eaters usually leave the crust behind. Cooking it in an Instant Pot Duo Evo Plus makes it come out more super creamy and silky. And if you refrigerate them, they can give you a cold breakfast or dinner dessert.

Total cook time: 21 minutes.

Ingredients

- 2 cups fresh pumpkin puree (or 2 cans pure pumpkin 15 oz.)
- 6 eggs
- 1 cup full fat coconut milk
- ¾ cup pure maple syrup (or light-colored raw honey)
- 1 tbsp. pumpkin pie spice
- ¾ tsp. finely grated lemon zest
- 2 tsp. pure vanilla extract
- ¼ tsp. sea salt
- 2 cups water

Instructions

1. Whisk together the first 8 ingredients up to and including sea salt. Evenly divide the mixture into 6 ramekins. Pour the lukewarm water into the Instant Pot and lower the wire rack. Cover the 6 ramekins tightly with silicone foil and set them on the rack.
2. Tightly secure the lid, ensuring that the steam release valve is set to the Sealing position. Select the Pressure Cook or Cake setting and turn the knob to set the cook time to 6 minutes (use the default time of cake if using the setting). When the pot beeps to signify the end of cook time, wait for 15-20 minutes of natural pressure release. When the pin drops, unlatch the lid to open the pot and remove the ramekins. Uncover the ramekins while still warm to avoid condensation build-up.
3. When the pies cool down to room temperature, cover the ramekins with plastic wraps and refrigerate for up to 5 days.

Yield: 6 servings.

Raspberry Steel Cut Baked Oatmeal Bars

Breakfast bars can be perfected if you use steel-cut oats as the base. It can be made with delicious raspberries where you will be treated with the tart flavor and the nutty flavor of the steel cut oats. There's also the chewy texture on your hand and mouth. Meanwhile, a fork can do the carriage.

Total cook time: 15 minutes.

Ingredients

- 3 cups steel-cut oats
- 3 large eggs
- 2 cups unsweetened vanilla almond milk
- 1/3 cup erythritol
- ¼ tsp. salt

- 1 cup frozen raspberries
- 1 tsp. pure vanilla extract
- 1 cup water

Instructions
1. Combine all ingredients except the raspberries and water in a medium bowl and mix thoroughly to combine well. Then, fold in the raspberries. Spray cooking pan with cooking oil and transfer the oat mixture to the pan. Cover slightly with aluminum foil.
2. Pour water into the Instant Pot with the steam rack inside. Position the pan containing the oat mixture on top of the rack.
3. Tightly secure the lid, ensuring that the steam release valve is set to the Sealing position. Select the Pressure Cook setting and program to cook for 15 minutes. When the timer beeps to signify the end of cook time, do a quick release of the pressure. When the float valve drops, unlatch the lid to open the pot and carefully remove the ramekins.
4. Remove the foil wait for a moment to cool completely. Then, cut into bars and serve.

Yield: 6 servings.

Nutrition content per serving: Calories: 399, Total Fat: 9g, Protein: 18g, Dietary Fiber: 12g Total Carbs: 72g.

Blueberry Almond Mason Jar Cakes

Blueberries are known for their antioxidant properties. They can fill foods with healthy nutrients for your body. The deep blue color is a sign that they contain powerful phytonutrients that help our body reduce the destruction by free radicals. Imagine gaining all of that in a delicious fruit package as a dessert.

Total cook time: 15 minutes.

Ingredients
- 4 large eggs
- 2 tsp. pure vanilla extract
- 1 1/3 cups almond flour
- ¼ cup erythritol
- 1 tsp. baking powder
- ¼ tsp. salt
- 1 cup blueberries
- ¼ cup sliced almonds

Instructions
1. Whisk the eggs and vanilla in a medium bowl and add the next four ingredients up to and including salt. Stir to combine. Then, fold in the blueberries.
2. Spray four glass of Mason jars with cooking oil and divide the batter into the jars. Next top each jar with parts of the almonds. Then, cover with aluminum foil.
3. Tightly secure the lid, ensuring that the steam release valve is set to the Sealing position. Select the Pressure Cook setting and program to cook for 15 minutes. When the timer beeps to signify the end of cook time, do a quick release of the

pressure. When the float valve drops, unlatch the lid to open the pot and carefully the pan ramekins.

4. Carefully remove the jars from the inner pot. Allow it to cool before serving.

Yield: 4 servings.

Nutritional content per serving: Calories: 345, Total Fat: 26g, Protein: 16g, Dietary Fiber: 6g, Carbohydrates: 28g.

Nutty Brownie Cake

When you're looking for a perfect slice of perfection, this nutty brownie cake is what you need. You'll find it handy during your craving for something chocolaty. Though small in stature, this recipe will satisfy the sweet tooth without leaving you with a sort of hangover the morning after.

.Total cook time: 20 minutes.

Ingredients

- 4 tbsp. butter room temperature
- 2 large eggs
- 1/3 cup all-purpose flour
- ½ tsp. baking powder
- 1/3 cup unsweetened cocoa powder
- Pinch of sea salt (to taste)
- 1/3 cup sugar
- 1/3 cup semisweet chocolate chips
- 1/3 cup chopped pecans
- 1 cup water
- 2 tbsp. powdered sugar

Instructions

1. Whisk together the first 7 ingredients including and up to sugar in a large bowl. Slightly mix and fold in chocolate chips and pecans. Pour the batter into a greased cake pan and cover with a piece of aluminum foil.
2. Pour the water into the pot and lower the trivet. Place the cake pan on top of the trivet in the pot. Tightly secure the lid, ensuring that the steam release valve is set to the Sealing position. Select the Pressure Cook setting and program to cook for 20 minutes. When the timer beeps to signify the end of cook time, do a quick release of the pressure. When the float valve drops, unlock the lid.
3. Transfer the cake from the pan to a rack to leave to cool. Serve sprinkling with powdered sugar.

Yield: 6 servings.

Oreo Cheesecake

We love and hate cheesecake at the same time. We love it so much so that people will hate how much we love it. Oreo is the culprit and takes the glory. However, it can be a nice way to end your breakfast and brighten your day. Welcome to the enjoyment of wholesome and hearty breakfast dessert to start your day with.

Total cook time: 1 hour.

Ingredients

- Cooking spray
- 26 Oreos (to be crushed, divided, plus more for garnish)
- 3 tbsp. melted butter
- Kosher salt (to taste)
- 2 blocks cream cheese (to be softened, 8 oz.)
- ½ cup granulated sugar
- ¼ cup packed brown sugar
- ¼ cup sour cream
- 2 large eggs
- 1 tsp. pure vanilla extract
- ¼ tsp. kosher salt
- 1 tbsp. all-purpose flour
- 1 cup water
- Cool whip for garnish
- Chocolate syrup for serving

Instructions

1. To make the crust, spray a springform pan with cooking spray. Combine 1½ cups of crushed Oreos, butter, and a pinch of salt in a medium bowl until the mixture feels like wet sand. Press it into the bottom and side of the pan and freeze for 20 minutes.
2. Meanwhile, use a hand mixer to beat cream cheese, sugars, and sour cream in a large bowl until light and fluffy. Add eggs and beat until blended. Add vanilla, salt, and flour. Beat until combined. Then fold in the remaining crushed Oreos. Pour the batter on top of the crust and tightly wrap the entire pan in two layers.
3. Add water into Instant Pot with trivet in the bottom. Position the springform pan on top.
4. Tightly secure the lid, ensuring that the steam release valve is set to the Sealing position. Select the Pressure Cook setting and program to cook for 37 minutes. When the timer beeps to signify the end of cook time, wait 10 minutes for a natural pressure release. Then do a quick release of the pressure. When the float valve drops, carefully unlock the lid.
5. Transfer the cheesecake from the pot to a wire rack. Unwrap and discard the foil. Then allow the cakes to cool for at least an hour and serve. It can be refrigerated for 4 hours or overnight. Serve garnished with cool whip, Oreos, or chocolate syrup.

Yield: 6 servings.

Fudgy Chocolate Cake

It's worth the while to conclude the section with a cake as a dessert. And it goes to the chocolate cake. Chocolate chips and cocoa powder are the differentiating factors in this recipe. But your friends won't know unless you tell them. Vanilla, butter, and eggs also play their usual role.

Total cook time: 30 minutes.

Ingredients
- 1 cup sugar

- 1 tsp. vanilla
- ½ cup butter
- 2 large eggs
- ¾ cup flour
- ½ cup cocoa powder
- 1 tsp. baking powder
- ½ tsp. salt
- 1 cup chocolate chips
- 1 cup water

Instructions

1. Use an electric mixer to cream the sugar, vanilla, and butter together in a large bowl until the mixture is light and fluffy. Add the eggs, one at a time. Beat thoroughly until well-combined.
2. Whisk together the flour, cocoa powder, baking powder, and salt in a small bowl. Slowly add the dry ingredients to the egg mixture and mix thoroughly until well-combined. Then stir in the chocolate chips.
3. Spray a springform pan with nonstick cooking spray. Ladle batter into the pan and smooth the top. Cover loosely with aluminum foil. Pour the water into the pot with wire trivet placed in the bottom. Set the pan on top.
4. Tightly secure the lid, ensuring that the steam release valve is set to the Sealing position. Select the Pressure Cook setting and program to cook for 30 minutes. When the timer beeps, wait 10 minutes for a natural pressure release. Then quickly release of the remaining pressure. When the float valve drops, carefully unlock the lid. Cut into wedges while still warm and serve.

Yield: 6 servings.

MEASUREMENT CONVERSIONS & ABBREVIATIONS

What determines how much you will enjoy the Instant Pot Duo is the extent to which you understand the measurements and abbreviations used in referring to its function. This chapter deals with that and a little addition to what has been said about the cooker in Chapter 1.

Note as said earlier that this Instant Pot comes in 6 quarts, and 8 quarts. As insignificant as the difference in sizes may be, it means a lot in cooking times. If the size of your recipe is bigger than the size of the Instant Pot, your food may not cook in the stipulated cook time. Also, note that bigger-size Instant Pot (Duo Evo Plus or not) takes longer to come to pressure. But when it comes to pressure, the cook time is constant if the power supply is constant.

Unless otherwise indicated in the recipe, the minimum water requirement for pressure cooking is as follows:

Size	Minimum Liquid requirement
6 quarts (5.7 liters)	1 ½ cups (12 oz. /376 ml)
8 quarts (7.6 liters)	2 cups (16 oz. /500 ml)

Inner Pot Diameter

Understanding the diameter of the inner pot is also crucial. It helps you to know the functionality of the Instant Pot.

- The diameter of the inner pot of 6 quarts Instant Pot is 8.5 inches
- The diameter of the inner pot of 8 quarts Instant Pot is 9.25 inches

Units of Measurement

The following abbreviations have been used as units of measurement. Beside them are there full meaning.

- Lb: Pounds
- Oz: Ounces
- Tsp.: teaspoon
- Tbsp.: tablespoon
- 1 cup = 16 tablespoons, 48 teaspoons
- 1 quart = 32 ounces

Understanding Instant Pot Duo Evo Plus Button

In case you want to experiment with the recipe by altering any of 100 recipes contained in this book, i is important that you understand the functions of buttons and keys on the pot. This will even give you a better idea of what each function will do for you and how long it will take.

1. **Soup/Broth:** The default time for this preset button is 30 minutes and it cooks at High Pressure. It cooks for 40 minutes when adjusted to more and 20 minutes when adjusted to less.

2. **Meat/Stew:** The default time for this preset button is 35 minutes and it cooks at High Pressure. It cooks for 45 minutes when adjusted to more and 20 minutes when adjusted to less.

3. **Bean/Chili:** The default time for this preset button is 30 minutes and it cooks at High Pressure. It cooks for 40 minutes when adjusted to more and 25 when adjusted to less.

4. **Poultry:** The default time for this preset button is 15 minutes and it cooks at High Pressure. It cooks for 30 minutes when adjusted to more and 5 minutes when adjusted to less.

5. **Rice:** The default time for this preset button is dependent on the quantity of water and rice in the pot. It is the only fully automatic and cooks at Low Pressure.

6. **Multigrain:** The default time for this preset button is 40 minutes and it cooks at High Pressure. It cooks for 45 minutes when adjusted to more and 20 minutes when adjusted to less.

7. **Porridge:** The default time for this preset button is 20 minutes and it cooks at High Pressure. It cooks for 30 minutes when adjusted to more and 15 minutes when adjusted to less.

8. **Steam:** The default time for this preset button is 10 minutes and it cooks at High Pressure. It cooks for 15 minutes when adjusted to more and 3 minutes when adjusted to less. You need this function when you have a rack or a steamer basket in the Instant Pot. It generates heat at full power continuously while coming to pressure. And it will prevent the food from having direct contact with the bottom of the pot. The steam button will regulate the pressure by cycling on and off when it is full.

9. **Less | Normal | More**: This button adjusts to Less, Normal, or More settings. You use it by pressing the same button for cooking function repeatedly until it reaches your desired setting.

10. **[-] and [+] Buttons**: This is used to program the cook time up "+" or down "-" if you press these buttons for 3 seconds on newer models, you are adjusting the sound to OFF or ON.

11. **Slow Cook:** This button adjusts the cooking temperature to 180 -190°F on low, 190 -200°F on normal, or 200 - 210°F on high.

12. **Pressure Level:** You can switch between High and Low Pressure settings.

13. **Keep Warm:** This automatically turns ON and OFF the Auto Keep Warm function. This will keep the contents of the Instant Pot warm at the temperature of 145 - 172°F.

14. **Yogurt:** You can adjust this to More to boil the milk, or to Normal to incubate the yogurt.

15. **Sauté:** This one of the most used buttons. While on the sauté mode, you have to wait until the message "Hot" is displayed on the display panel before you start adding ingredients to the pot. Adjust to Normal for sautéing veggies, to More for browning meats, and adjust to Less for simmering.

16. **Delay Start:** This is used to select a cooking function and adjustments. After mixing all the ingredients and you don't want the cooking to start immediately, press the Delay Start and use the [+] and [-] buttons to program how long you'd like the Instant Pot to wait before starting the cooking.

17. **Cancel:** This button terminates a cooking program at any time. If you press and hold this key the Instant Pot will beep to reset to factory settings (This is not the case on all models. In fact, on the Ultra, doing so returns you to the previous step where you selected your cooking options.)

18. **Pressure Cook:** This is the most commonly used key. You can select the Pressure Level to switch between Low and High Pressure. You can also use [+] or [-] to adjust cook time. The timer will start to countdown when pressure is reached.

When Living on High Altitude

There may be a slight or significant difference in the cook times from what is stated in the recipe depending on the altitude you are cooking at. The air pressure is lower at a higher elevation and that brings a lot of alterations in cook time with it.

1. The boiling point of water is lower, so food will cook at a lower temperature and takes more time.

2. The rate of evaporation of liquids is higher; so liquid: grain or liquid: flour ratio needs to be changed.

3. Gases expand rapidly; so baking will happen faster, so also leavening.

The chart below helps to explain what is obtainable at different altitudes:

Altitude (in feet)	% of the increase in cook time	For 20 min. recipes	For 60 min. recipes
3,000	5	21 min.	63 min.
4,000	10	22 min.	66 min.
5,000	15	23 min.	66 min.
6,000	20	24 min.	69 min.
7,000	25	25 min.	72 min.
8,000	30	26 min.	75 min.
9,000	35	27 min.	78 min.

ABBREVIATIONS AND ERROR CODES

Even though certain expressions abbreviated were spelled out in this book, it's also possible to come across other abbreviations in the text explaining or commenting on the Instant Pot Duo Evo Plus. The commonest of them have been explained below, listed in alphabetical order.

1. **EPC:-** Electric Pressure Cooker. The Instant Pot Evo Duo Plus is one of these.
2. **HA:-** High Altitude. How high the location of the cooking influences how soon the Instant Pot will reach pressure and the total cook time. If you are living in high altitudes, say about 3,000 ft. above sea level, you need to adjust the total cook times for most recipes.
3. **HP:-** High Pressure. Any pressure level from 10.2 - 11.6 psi is considered high.
4. **IP:-** This is a short form of Instant Pot also known as Magic Pot.
5. **LP:** -Low Pressure. Any pressure level from 5.8 - 7.2. Your pot is cooking at low pressure if it's cooking at this pressure level.
6. **NR:-** Natural Release. You do a natural pressure when you allow the Instant Pot Duo Evo Plus to release the pressure inside after the cook time without touching it. When the pressure is all gone, the floating valve/steam release handle will naturally drop eventually.
7. **NPR:-** Natural Pressure Release. The same as NR.
8. **Pothead:-** This is a slang used to describe the Instant Pot users. Another variation is potters.
9. **PC:-** Pressure Cookers. It's the general description of all pots that cook with high pressure.
10. **PIP:-** Pot-in-Pot / Pan-in-Pan. If you're in a hurry and you want to cook two or more dishes with the same cook time at the same time in one Instant Pot Duo Evo Plus, you can use PIP. Just make sure the pots are oven-safe.

11. **PSI**:- Pound Per Square Inch. This is the unit of measurement of atmospheric pressure required for pressure cooking.
12. **QPR:-** Quick Pressure Release. Another expression for QR.
13. **QR:-** Quick Release. This is also referred to as Manual Release. As explained in Chapter 1, you do QR or QPR when you turn the venting knob/ handle/ valve/ steam release from the sealing position to the venting position. It allows all the pressure to be quickly or manually release and allows the pin to drop faster.
14. **SB**:- Steamer Basket. This is what you use to steam foods inside the Instant Pot Duo Evo Plus.
15. **SS**:- Stainless Steel. The stainless steel is what is used to make the cooking area of the Instant Pot Duo Evo Plus.
16. **7-7-7**: High Pressure: 7 minutes, Natural Pressure Release: 7 Minutes, Ice Bath: 7 Minutes. You say this when you're recommending the timing for the cooking certain foods, such as quail eggs. It may also be given as 5-5-5.

Error Codes and Meaning

When an error occurs on the Instant Pot Duo Evo Plus, it will stop functioning instead of continuing to cook and cause serious damage. Meanwhile, it will beep continuously until it is attended to. Before you disconnect it, however, check the display panel and see the code displayed. It might be a minor error that you can correct.

Below are the examples of such errors and what you can do about them.

Error	Meaning	Solution
C1, C2, C6, C6H, C6L	Faulty sensor	Contact Customer Care
C7, NoPr	1. Heat element has failed 2. Not enough liquid 3. Quick-release switch left in the Vent position	For 1, contact Customer Care For 2, Add water or thin, water-based liquid to the pot until it reaches the minimum requirement for the recipe based on the size as explained earlier
C8	Wrong inner pot in the cooker base.	Insert the inner pot with the right size and easy-grip handles into the cooker base
Lid	The lid is not in the correct position for your selected program	1. Open and close the lid back. 2. Don't use a lid when on Sauté function

OvHt / Burn / Food burn	An unusually high temperature detected at the bottom of the inner pot; the cooker automatically reduces the temperature to prevent overheating	The heat dissipation may have been blocked by the starch deposits at the bottom of the inner pot. Turn the cooker off and release the pressure as the recipe directs. Then inspect the bottom of the inner pot
PrSE	An accumulation of pressure during a non-pressure cooking program	Quickly turn the steam release switch valve to the Vent position

CONCLUSION

The last time you cooked in the Instant Pot, you no doubt felt and believed that your cooking has reached the next level. You could then relate to what many folks have been talking about regarding the convenience, versatility, cleanness, sleekness, and speed of the Instant Pot. There you're! Welcome to the new world of cooking!

After gaining a full understanding of the functionality of the Instant, I could hardly imagine anyone asking for anything more in pressure cooking. It seems to have got all you need for pressure cooking. However, aren't we Oliver Twist?

That's the essence of a series of generational changes in the Instant Pot. From generation to generation, improvements have been made. Those improvements definitely improve the user's experiences with the Instant Pot. Besides these generational improvements, new models are being made.

The Instant Pot Duo Evo Plus has come to rule its predecessors. It will take a while before it can be beaten.

Printed in Great Britain
by Amazon

25437636R00061